The Domestic Archaeologist

Confessions of a Professional Home Declutterer

The Domestic Archaeologist

Confessions of a Professional Home Declutterer

Stephen Ilott

IGUANA

Copyright © 2017 Stephen Ilott
Published by Iguana Books
720 Bathurst Street, Suite 303
Toronto, Ontario, Canada
M5S 2R4

All rights reserved. No part of this publication may be reproduced, stored in a retrieval system or transmitted, in any form or by any means, electronic, mechanical, recording or otherwise (except brief passages for purposes of review) without the prior permission of the author or a licence from The Canadian Copyright Licensing Agency (Access Copyright). For an Access Copyright licence, visit www.accesscopyright.ca or call toll free to 1-800-893-5777.

Publisher: Mary Ann J. Blair
Editor: Jen R. Albert
Front cover image: Stephen Ilott

ISBN 978-1-77180-233-8 (paperback)
ISBN 978-1-77180-234-5 (EPUB)
ISBN 978-1-77180-235-2 (Kindle)

This is an original print edition of *The Domestic Archaeologist*.

For my wife, Irene.

She knows how long it really took me to evolve (if I ever did), and put up with it.

Contents

Foreword xi

Preface: This Book Is About My Journey xv

Part One:
The Domestic Archaeologist 1

  Why a Domestic Archaeologist? 1

  Letting Go of the Balloon 2

  House Sneaky Is That? 5

  Why More Ladies than Men? 8

  That's Where That Is! 10

  The Domestic Archaeologist Redefined 11

  Choose Your Battles 15

  New Normals 18

  What I Do Is Who I Am 20

Part Two:
Spring, the Vernal Equinox of Life 24

  I Smell Burnt Toast 25

  Multi-Multi-Tasking 26

  Small Words Reverberate Large 27

  I'm Tired of This Game — Let's Play Another 28

  We Are Delicate Machines 29

  Don't Burn the Bridge – You May Need the Lumber
  Later On. 31

  Spring into the Unexpected Journey 33

The UP Button and the Hero Mindset............................35
Be off Trajectory on Purpose...36
Guinea Pigs Can Fly 38
True Fiction 39
My First Lessons: The Calls of the Wild 40
I'm a Realtor — Info Me Up 42
Opportunivores 47
Smitten Detectives 52
Careful Sifting 54
Can I Ask You — On a Scale of One to Ten…..............55
Lessons About Patience from a Rocky Start.................55
Absence Makes the Heart Grow Flounder....................57
The Game's the Thing 58
Lessons on Overthink 60
Parallel Normals 65
    Shoes 65
    Dust...67
    Stuffed Toys 71
Poke Some Holes 72
Be at the Helm of Change So You Can Enjoy It When It Happens...73
Can Daddy Move Us to a Neat House? 74
Be Aware When Things Leave Your Hand 77
The Thirty Second Rule..78
The Thirty Second Rule and Focus................................81
Garage Sale Confidential..82

    The Outdoor Store 88

    Flash Mob Two-Step 92

    Scrappers 93

    Spring Takeaways 94

Part Three:
Summer Solstice and the Season of the Strange 95

    A Two-Chicken Day 96

    Smile, You're on Candid Camera 97

    It's a Guy Thing 99

    I Can Hear the Chickens Calling: Bark, Bark, Bark,
    Bark, Bark, Bark, Meow….. 101

    Cat on a Hot Tinnitus Roof 104

    All That Jazz 109

    The Fruit Fly House 114

    Here's My Cigar — What's Your Hurry? 119

    Keep Your Back to the Sun, Eh? 121

    The Two-Chicken Day Lectures 126

        The Charity Event Lecture 128
        The Switching Directions Lecture 130
        The "Where Are You?" Lecture 130
        The Baffled Audience Lecture 131
        The Flax Lecture 132

    Lords of the Hoards 135

    Summer Takeaways 142

Epilogue: The Cat's Breakfast 145

Acknowledgements 147

Foreword

by Rick Green

In your hands right now you are holding a most unusual, intriguing, and powerful book about organizing and decluttering. (You may also be holding a gun, bullwhip, triple shot of booze, or a handful of tranquilizers. You can put those other things down. All you'll need is this book.)

The Domestic Archeologist does what any good archeologist does, digging through the accumulated layers of detritus to uncover the patterns and life that have been lost over time. This isn't about mummies and pyramids. It's about reclaiming your life from the billion things and to-dos that have buried you alive.

And it's a hoot.

Now, I know there are lots of books about getting organized and decluttering. I used to have many of them. They're somewhere, mixed in with broken toasters, some perfectly good Halloween decorations someone was throwing out, and 153 boxes of model trains.

Now all I have is Stephen Ilott's book. (And thirty boxes of model trains, all organized and labelled.)

What makes this book special, beyond the strange last name of the author (it's either Finnish or Martian ... I forget ... he told me once), is ... where was I? (Sorry, did I mention I met Stephen at an ADHD Conference? No? I did. We bonded right away. Well, he did. I thought he was way too cheerful and was going to hand me a religious pamphlet.)

Anyways, my point is ... Sorry, I forgot where I was ... Oh, right.

In this book, Stephen asks us to dig into our lives. Not just our physical junk, but our emotional and mental rubble that has brought us to the point where we've bought a book on organizing. (If you haven't bought this book, do so now. Making the decision to buy the book will be the first of many decisions you'll make in getting rid of what you don't want so you can focus on what you love.)

Sorry, I wandered again, didn't I?

The Domestic Archeologist asks us to look beyond the clutter to see the bigger picture, the bigger context, and our bigger goals. Not our bucket list, which is often just a list of exotic destinations and wild thrills, but what we want our lives to be.

Stephen has us ask, "Why do I want that?" (And yes, what you want will be different from what I want. Your 153 boxes may contain Star Wars memorabilia, Hummel figurines, mystery novels, or needlepoint supplies. All blended together with a million bits of crap.)

It wasn't always like this, was it? Heck it wasn't this bad two months ago. And it's not getting better.

We were younger and more confident about what we liked.

Then the world bombarded us with ads, flyers, commercials, products, courses, goals, to-dos, widgets, trends, fads, and the endless torrent of new techno-gadgets that make last month's version an obsolete piece of garbage that we can't stand using because it takes an extra 1.835 seconds to launch Facebook.

Why? Because it will make someone money.

By promising to make you happier.

Once upon a time you didn't need a pasta maker to be happy. Your wants and goals were cleaner, clearer, and more powerful. They were more true to who you were, or who you wanted to be when you grew up.

Stephen Ilott is not the first person to notice that our lives have spiralled out of control. He is not the first to point out that clutter fills more than our cupboards, closets, basements and storage units; it also fills our schedules, finances, computer desktops, agendas, and wish lists.

Stephen may be the first person to offer us both big picture strategies to clarify what we want our lives to look like, and then provide ideas and structures for us to distill our lives down to what is essential to each of us in such a unique way.

Best of all, he does it with humour and patience, warmth, wit, and generosity. And he's not paying me fifty bucks to say that! LOL.

What makes Stephen so great in real life is what makes this book so great; he likes people, he loves making a difference, he's generous, warm, witty, and patient. He seems to radiate trust and confidence that everything will work out.

And guess what, with Stephen helping, it always does.

Enjoy!

(Hey Stephen, here's the intro. You owe me fifty bucks for lying like this. Send the money and never contact me again or I'll call the cops.) (And for God's sake don't forget to remove this part before you send it to the printer. Oh, and Ava says, "Give our love to Irene.")

Rick Green — co-founder of TotallyADD.com., creator of History Bites, contributor to The Red Green Show, *recipient of the Order of Canada and a ton of other stuff too.*

Preface: This Book Is About My Journey

Like just about everyone, I am a hog for a good story. There's a reason. We glean our life lessons from stories, as they are full of inspiration and secret, vicarious joys. Reading about others somehow connects us all. We all have stories. Stories surround us. What is advertising, if not little stories to glom on to? We look for stories in old photographs of long-lost people and wonder what that person's story was, or what happened the moment after the shot was taken and onwards. We love images of roads winding into the distance and long to follow them just to see where they go. We love photographs of doors and want to step inside, wondering who and what we will find. We long to escape our own lives and our mistaken belief that a big house means happiness. As my sage wife often says, as we pass mansions in our town of Oakville, Ontario, on our way to our humble abode, "But they're not happy."

The joy of my world and business is that I am privy to an abundance of stories — the warp and woof of life in all its tangled glory.

I have travelled many roads these past fifteen years, both real and imagined. On the downside, I've been injured, insulted, and had lit cigars flicked at me. On the upside, thankfully, I have been praised and applauded for my efforts and hard work and been drawn close to realtors and homeowners who value me as the asset they toss into the fray. I grew, unwittingly, along with my clients, some of whom became fast friends.

I am still growing. After I finished writing this book I had changed again, remembering things forgotten, dusted off and set on a shelf to look at again. It also helped me remember how I got into this crazy business and why I stayed in it.

So, OK, this isn't so much an organizing book as it is about me finding my elusive purpose in life and how that journey served so many other lives. Each season brought me closer to finding the meaning of life. Read on and you may find yours in learning how I found mine. One certainty is that I needed to grow up, need to grow up, will need to grow up some more. It begins as any book of change, motivation, and inspiration should begin — at the beginning. I use seasons as metaphors, as certain kinds of experiences have happened to me in specific times of year: spring, summer, autumn, and winter. Some of my stories also reflect the stage of my decluttering career that I was experiencing at the time. In the spring of my career I was fresh and green, and eager for change and new growth. And although there are many more chapters to unfold in the years ahead, and I am still a (relatively) young man at this juncture, I consider my career to be in the "autumn" phase of things now — I am wise (sometimes) and mature, with a trove of stories that only wizened ears and mileage under the belt can appreciate.

Reading any book, you become someone other than who you were before you started reading. You may also recognize what season you are in. I look forward to change each day when I wake up, hoping it's a good one. Life is change, and I use heaping dollops of humour because I wouldn't have achieved nearly as much without it, nor retained my sanity. If you haven't got a sense of humour, stop reading now, and go buy a book about sparkly teenage vampires.

My world will make you laugh the way it makes me laugh, and sometimes it will make you cry in the way it has made me cry. Yes, I cry, my first confession.

A second confession is that I can't ignore retelling some of my stories any more than I can ignore a trouser full of scrabbling weasels. They're part of me now. Oh yeah, I have a babbly sense of humour as you may have guessed, and I love words. An old Arab phrase tells us, "The tongue has no bones but it can crush." I like to think the tongue can tickle just as much. I meant that words can tickle just as much ... OK, stop smiling you savage rascal.

I've been promising these books for a dog's age now, putting them off for years and for many of the same no-good reasons most writers wrestle with, as well as some reasons that surprised me when they revealed themselves. Only now can I say I wrote it down the way I wanted to. And instead of battling any demons or fears I may have had about writing down my adventures, I simply invited them to lunch. The truth is, now I've stopped enabling my own inner naysayer. The gaps and delays in between seemed to have had a purpose. If you have ever had a good chat with yourself to find out what's going on, you'll know what I mean. There are more confessions inside, if you care to take a peek. I already have a sequel in me, gestating like an alien about to pop out and spoil everyone's lunch — or rather it's the continuance of the journey. Or it could just be that second pesto chicken souvlaki combo I had at my favourite pita joint.

So, curl up on the couch, pop a nice bottle of plonk, cue the fireplace, and turn to the next page and grow with me.

Stephen Ilott, Oakville, Ontario, Canada

Part One: The Domestic Archaeologist

Why a Domestic Archaeologist?

I am a Domestic Archaeologist. It might sound like a nervous admission made in a room full of scraping chairs or the first words in a Discovery Channel documentary, but it's actually a clarification of sorts. I find the title "Professional Organizer" somewhat dry, lacking a certain depth of emotion. It also seems to fill everyone I tell it to with violent apathy, probably because it's about as evocative as saying, "I toss cheese to squirrels."

"Domestic Archaeologist," by contrast, tickles the brain and inspires curiosity. You can't keep yourself from responding. It's like trying to say the word "bubbles" without grinning like a nutter. You can't do it. Go on, I can wait. Bubbles ... bubbles.

Even in casual conversation, the term "Professional Organizer" doesn't have that eager, tell-me-more factor. "Declutterer" is closer to the mark, and that suits me just fine, but it also makes me sound a tad like a charity junk man. Decluttering speaks to emotion and history, and the letting go of moments and things that are no longer useful. Decluttering your life implies that something has changed or has to change. That can be invigorating, inspiring, cathartic, and scary. Decluttering also focuses your mind, lest some treasured memory be lost. It emphasizes the act of selecting the much-loved over the less-loved, and it evokes the painful certainty of separation from something that was once part of you but is now redundant — for better or for worse.

Letting Go of the Balloon

I use the term "Declutterer" for clarity and "Domestic Archaeologist" for impact (DomArch for short). I stopped introducing myself as a Professional Organizer when I realized the impact the vague term had on people: their eyes would glaze over and narrow like they'd been sniffing glue; time would slow down, and their heads would tilt like a puppy tuning into a high-frequency whistle. And when their mouths scrunched into a lemon-drop pucker, I knew we'd hit the letting-go-of-the-balloon moment. Their you've-just-lost-me look made me wonder if they thought I had just been unexpectedly barking at them in Icelandic. I often had to beep-beep-back-it-up and say it again, only simpler, as if I were talking earnestly to a goldfish.

I pictured the poor sod in question holding a shiny pink balloon ribbon between pincer-like fingers. Their pupils would dilate, their pincers would open, and the balloon would drift to the ceiling, taking their ability to speak along with it. On very special days, I could almost imagine a puff of blue smoke wafting from their ears for effect.

People were generally too embarrassed to actually say, "Huh, sooo you do … zzzzt … zzzt … what?"

"I am a Professional Home Organizer," I would repeat for the benefit of those bold enough to ask for clarification. This time I would mouth the words like I was trying out French for the first time in public. To their credit, they would try, momentarily, to understand, then the vacant look that took hold of their faces usually told me I was wasting my energy, and in mere seconds, they would drift away like their balloons.

Sometimes people would say, "That's nice," and escape quickly to the cannoli, leaving me with the feeling that I was in possession of my own special stun ray that was triggered by speech.

I've run into that reaction a good deal over the years and am now an expert in its pathology. The letting-go-of-the-balloon moment is not unlike like the frozen stare you get when chatting with someone who's waiting for their turn to speak. Time-starved real estate agents, a special breed, have a talent for that one. If you've stepped into the orbit of a realtor in the past few years, by accident or by intention, you'll know that they've honed their moments to absolutes. Time is money. Fingernails drum tabletops. The fleeting courtesy look they bestow on you at no extra charge implies that the clock is ticking, so get on with it because your verbal credit is just about up. Lawyers are equally adept at that, along with bored teenage store clerks, gas station attendants, and anybody with twitchy fingers, furtive eyes, and an urgent need to send a text message.

It strikes me that this type of unspoken dismissal is the scourge of modern life. You can't take it personally. People don't get enough face time with others nowadays, so everybody talks in clips and spurts — a type of shorthand that leaps about between unfinished and unfulfilled sentences. We have to impress each other in mere milliseconds and bedazzle with panache. I once started to speak to a realtor who prefaced my coming words with, "You have ten seconds, go big or go home." She said it with a beguiling smile. It strikes me that lurking behind many a smile are preemptive thoughts waiting to pounce.

I wish things weren't that way, but sadly, they seem to be tobogganing in that direction at great speed. Worse, you have to repeat everything you say now because everyone is so tuned in to their own lurking thoughts and weighted words.

All of which is a long way of saying that, when time and patience are in short supply, I dump the term "Professional Organizer" in favour of the more descriptive "Declutterer." The word is instantaneously understood and the response it generates is much more to my liking. Decluttering, in fact, has become the buzzword of our time. It holds people's interest long enough for me to add that I organize people's lives and motivate them and, yes, I do this for a living, full-time. I help them let go of the bad past and safeguard the good past. I unburden them of the emotion-laden stuff they've mounded around themselves like a big pile of autumn leaves.

Sometimes I say, "Husbands call me in to organize their wife's stuff." That's a gob-smacking biggie. Husbands calling in an outsider and paying for what their wives should be doing for free? Nah, baloney! Tell me more.

Worse still is the reaction I get from men when I explain that wives sneak me in to organize their husband's stuff. I mean, a house is a castle — nay a fortress — a privileged, albeit cluttered, sanctuary. One doesn't just invade a man cave and shovel a guy's junk … I mean you simply can't ... can you? "And somebody pays you to ... good lord..." Balloons of disbelief bounce gaily on the ceiling at that point, big red ones.

I love it when the moment of understanding comes and people get what I do. It's usually followed by one of three excited reactions:

1) "Oh my god, you actually do that for a living? I didn't think anybody actually did that! Wow, everybody needs you!"

Or

2) "Damn, where were you last year when I sold my house?"

Or

3) "My husband would never let you in the front door. Really, never, ever ... ever! Run away now before he hears you. Here he comes now. Run! Too late. Pretend I know you from Hot Yoga."

Once in a while, they lean into me conspiratorially, eyes darting from side to side, and whisper things, like "My sister should have you over. Yeah, seriously, she lives like a slug."

House Sneaky Is That?

Understanding what I do is one thing, but inviting me into a private space of shame is another. Somewhere along the way, I learned to soft-step into my client's rhythms. It's as if people are asking me, a complete stranger, to share their secrets. It's sensitive stuff. Upon arriving on a client's porch, I sometimes expect a small slit of a panel to slide sideways on the door and a pair of inquisitive eyes to ask me for the password. The password would, of course, be "declutter." After furtively ushering me in, some women even check the streets, as though they're engaged in some subversive behaviour, like sharing secrets with the Russians or planning to rope their neighbours into a new multi-level marketing scheme.

Now and then, a client will ask me if I have a sign on my car, not just because they're worried about what their husbands would do if they knew what I was up to but also in case the neighbours catch a glimpse. If I say yes, I am urgently requested to park down the street. Clearly, organizers and declutterers still have some PR work to do before we earn the cachet of the Home & Garden-style house stager. Truth be told, most neighbours are buried deep in their own private clutter, with at least one embarrassing room, basement, shed, attic, or cringe-worthy closet.

There's a *Dangerous Liaisons* aspect to being called in to declutter someone's home, which adds a bit of lustre to the job. I can't help but smile when I hear in a hushed whisper, "He won't be home for hours. Let's go at it." I feel like the milkman in a Monty Python sketch and imagine having to be frog-marched unceremoniously into an armoire at the unexpected jangling of keys at the front door.

You think I kid, but one afternoon, after an extensive basement rework, I had to sneak past a client's family when they came home early. Upon hearing creaking floor boards and murmurs of movement from above, my client stiffened like a rabbit. Her index fingers shot to either side of her head like she was receiving a telepathic message. This confused me, and I asked, "Do you have a headache?" She shush-blurted that I had to leave right away and "be very, very quiet." I giggled as her words came out, in my mind at least, in a raspy whisper, à la Elmer Fudd.

Creeping your way up squeaking basement steps and across an open hallway like a cat burglar with a bag of tools in tow is not as easy as you might think. More cartoon images came to mind as I tippy toed my way toward the door and I half expected to hear the pizzicato plucking of a violin string from a Warner Brothers cartoon. You wouldn't believe how sensitive people are in those situations. They sense things: soundless vibrations, a stirring in the air, eyes boring into their backs. Women and girls pick that up in a jiffy and their heads snap your way with laser accuracy. If my client's daughter had been the one coming home early that day, the jig would have been up in a heartbeat. Thankfully, it was only her two teenage boys and the dreaded hubby. Boys could look directly at a rhinoceros ambling across the vestibule, but unless it was packing a ham sandwich, they wouldn't notice it. The tricky part was the front door. When I got to it, I did an about-face, felt the door handle behind me, opened it ever so gingerly, and backed my way out fast. When faces turned, I waved as if poking my head in just to say, "I'm picking up those recyclables now, Mrs." How she explained that part I never knew. I wasn't asked back.

Women definitely feel a private shame around hiring an organizer. They are embarrassed by the accumulation, by the fact that they can't face how or where to start, and, above all else, by the fact that life didn't go off as planned. Life loses its thread, and there is a deep, palpable longing to get life back on track, or even to return to how things used to be. Finding where that thread of life unravelled is an important goal for every person I help motivate.

Even when a woman has finally worked up the courage to bring in an outsider like me to help her move forward, she often has to circumnavigate the grumpy, territorial overlord who'll whip out his huffing tricoloured invectives at the drop of a baseball cap. Yes, husbands are the bane of every organizer's existence. Many of us have seen a solid prospect poof into air with not a whisper of explanation. If a man's home is his castle, his collections of ancient, yellowed, dusty artifacts — like every decrepit computer, keyboard, and mouse he's ever owned (along with the boxes and mildewed Styrofoam) are his crown jewels. Decluttering those "treasures" amounts to a declaration of war. One learns to tread lightly where men are concerned.

Why More Ladies than Men?

I may have more stories about women than men. Truly, this is a field that is teeming with the heroic adventures of the female gender. I find older women are woefully underserved by the reality TV universe and its ever-narrowing, subdismal gaze, filled with impossibly coiffed, crackly-voiced twenty-somethings fuming about their lack of shoe space and their dated countertops. Their husbands, meanwhile, are depicted as clueless, arm-flapping mouth-breathers enthralled by big-screen TVs and sweater puppies.

The older ladies, I find, have given their all and then some, and sometimes feel as if life, appreciation, and time have gone on a tear without them. I love their common and very urgent need to cultivate, reinvent, and enrich their lives, and have a really elegant lunch in the process. They also have a refreshing maturity and a wicked sense of humour. It's an earned position after the price they pay for a full life, to badly paraphrase Sofia Loren. At a networking meeting I once attended, one member announced it was her twenty-sixth birthday again. Another woman of similar vintage chimed in with, "Yeah, twenty-six plus tax." Older women want to set their worlds on fire, even as they joke about their own internal combustion engines monkeying with the thermostat. They are defiance and self-deprecation all balled into one and served up with a twinge of sea salt. I like that. It makes them a grand, appreciative audience for the mirror I hold up during my many lectures.

That sentiment was underpinned by Patsy, a wonderful childhood friend of mine. She lamented the quickening surge of years going by. It struck her one morning as she was dropping her teenage boys off at yet another urgent sports event. It was too early to permit time for her customary makeup ministrations, as was the case with every other drop-off mom she encountered. She said, "I found myself suddenly surrounded by this Halloween horror ... this sorority of old broads, and I fit right in." Perhaps it's that poignant quality that makes me want to be a woman's ally in reinvention. Maybe it's the Irish in me that appreciates pointed real-life humour sprinkled generously with equal doses of melancholy and regret.

As a male, I am an extreme rarity in my profession. I used to be a membership director for a national group of organizers I am fond of, called the Professional Organizers in Canada (POC). There were some 700 members at the time and only about six guys. I am surrounded by women who are amazed that I exist in this business at all. Why should that be? Why shouldn't a guy be as empathetic, sympathetic, and patient as a woman, or at least be seen to be? Being a male gives me a different relationship with my clients, one where expectations are uncharted and results are hugely appreciated. I also understand both sides of the couple equation. While men reluctantly follow my lead and eventually thank me, reserving the right to pee the perimeter at any moment, women are game to have me in and they are enthusiastic about trying the new perspectives I offer. A big reason is that the decluttering of a home inevitably falls upon the women of the family. They are the default archivists entrusted with the task of safeguarding memories. In the case of sisters — the job often falls on the shoulders of the eldest daughter.

Now and then, having a male organizer on hand offers women a chance to posit theories as to why a brother or father acted in a certain way, then pick my brain on ways to motivate the males in their family to come around to their way of thinking.

That's Where That Is!

The real fun begins when I find something a client thought was long lost, especially something that was a big part of who they used to be. It sparks a memory that jolts them right back to a special moment in time. Lost innocence often surfaces in the unearthing of past family moments. Seeing clients crumple at the memory of times long gone is moving beyond words. Sometimes, rediscovery flares into a renewal of an old interest and the hope of maybe becoming that person again, the person they missed being. This is at the heart of longing and loss. Reaching into the past to help reinvent your future can be powerful, no matter what season of life you find yourself in: spring or summer (my themes for this book) or autumn or winter (the themes for my next one).

I help people move forward — "the very forward," as I call it. I help them live life less large and more Zen, and I offer my nickel-plated nuggets of wisdom along the way. The freedom that comes with letting go of stuff always seems to surprise people. Being free of something they didn't know was holding them down is eye-opening. Sometimes I can tell them what that something was; often, it's for them to discover, a private, satisfying revelation.

Not everyone is cut out for decluttering their life. It's not for sissies. It takes courage to look in the mirror, accept what you see, and let go of self-defeating habits and stuff so you can move on. Sometimes it starts with a tiny push, like with those little wind-up toys, weeblies or wobblies, or whatever they're called — the ones that scissor down an incline without a care in the world faster and faster until they fall over sideways, still grinning.

My world is as much about exploring a different kind of unknown as it is about giving advice and hauling "get-rid-ables" to charity. I never know who I'll deal with next. I take a deep breath before each doorstep, and not just because the air may be less than tickety-boo inside. It's all an adventure, and it's fascinating to me. Since we are all notorious custodians of stuff, there's never a lack of it to deal with, and there's always someone to put new energy into all that stuff once I've hauled it away.

The Domestic Archaeologist Redefined

These are reparable times. Everything in our lives is in dire need of patching, retrofitting, and all-out tweaking. This includes our relationships, finances, and certainly the place we call Home Sweet Home. The emergence of service industries, such as professional organizing, arose from our growing need for allies to get us back on track. We increasingly yearn for someone to step into our unfocused world so we can point to what we have wrought and say, "Look at it. Just look at it!"

Did we always need someone else to organize our lives so deeply but just didn't realize it? Did we always have this tango-dance existence of two steps forward and one step back, leaving us with an unsatisfied feeling of not quite getting things done as fast and as well as we had hoped? Certainly, the speeding up of time and technology has squeezed true family and friends to the sidelines. Traditionally those were the people we could count on for a wake-up call. They've been replaced by "Bitmap Humans" — digital stranger-friends, ersatz pals who can be unfriended with the flick of a thumb. Maybe the increasing reliance on professional organizers shows a return to inviting real flesh and blood people into our lives again, for guidance. With all the scampering about to keep up with an escalating world where outside optics is all, inside home maintenance has fallen seriously out of whack. To make matters worse, too many people have forgotten, or never learned, remedial organizational skills. It is the stuff that takes slow, deliberate, methodical effort to achieve. Nobody has time for slow or deliberate any more, let alone methodical. There's too much to keep up with, to sort through, to assess, leaving us in a perpetual state of feeling behind.

Technology helps many etch their presence into the remorseless passage of time (especially for women), but too much cataloguing can also steal the very moment one wants to hold on to. Something is always missing in the Facebook update or the Instagram I'm-out-there-living-life selfie of the day, something deeper. We are the last generation that looked up. No one sees the flowers, let alone stops to smell them anymore — something technology cannot supply. I miss the visceral validation of a passing stranger, no matter the culture or language, and their momentary scrunched-up, slightly demented grin that says, "Hey there, other human, I'm safe and not wielding an axe; scrunch-smile me back will ya?" Human reconnection is a close-proximity thing, not a facsimile image mailed off by pressing "Send," smiley face.

And life/work balance? Nah! That doesn't exist either. The best balance we can hope for is to live vicariously, carving out a few addicted hours watching unreality TV shows like *House Hunters International* (a personal favourite). Can you say an apartment in Paris? Mais-non!

As a result of our lack of balance and time, and our desperate need for the unreachable intangible, our abodes are just plain messy. It is the new norm. Messy fills the empty spaces where time and lives lost traction.

Yet that very same yearning is a good thing, forcing change. A growing number of folks are reaching out to professional organizers, partly because of an increased sense of isolation and partly because so many people need a good jolt to initiate forward momentum for their own sweet good. And a growing number of people simply don't know where to start or how to help a family member or parent mired in years of clutter. Our job prospectus is rewritten each time we dig into the lives of our clients to discover where things fell apart, or simply stopped, and why nobody is doing anything about it. It is Domestic Archaeology redefined.

Certainly, more clients than ever are calling me in, just to nail them in place long enough to get something — anything — done before the phone rings or an urgent text hijacks them into a rapid-fire thumb-twiddling frenzy. "Just gotta answer this, answer this, answer this…"

When I began my organizing business, what I saw was just the tip of the iceberg. I had no clue what an unexpectedly off-kilter world I was dipping into. Professional home organizing in those days was still about organizing the home, the ergonomics of use. Now it is far more about organizing lives or, as that one client put it, helping her find the thread of her life. She had lost the thread. My tagline of "Therapy for Your Home" quickly became "Therapy for the Homeowner."

The original term "Domestic Archaeologist" applied to the study of ancient archaeological ruins, though few people actually call themselves one (a Domestic Archaeologist, not a ruin) save for me, as far as I know. There will be more of us; of that I have no doubt. House ruination isn't just an ancient occurrence, no indeedy. We all have degrees of it, from the slip-sliding piles of glossy flyers promoting things you'll never buy to the ubiquitous junk drawer — that elephant graveyard of everything small and completely useless: ancient grocery receipts; broken pencils; dead batteries; the bulbless flashlight; yard-long purple produce elastics; the small ceramic toothpick barrel, in blue or brown, filled with lint; safety pins and crooked paper clips; a cracked and yellowed plastic jar of flat metal thumb tacks; a baggie full of bread bag ties; knotted string; a screw driver without bits; out-of-date coupons to restaurants you'd never eat at; cheap packing tape whose edge was next to invisible so you gave up trying to find it; the "how in heck did that get in there?" item; and at least one of those gadgets you bought off TV that fell apart the moment you touched it, so you went out and bought another one. Which then also broke.

The junk drawer is the repository of all things temporary, our deferred detritus. When plunging a hand into one, we hesitate momentarily over the abyss, fingers curled and tingling with the memories of an unexpected paper cut, pin prick, or under-the-fingernail jab from a loose staple. Does anyone ever vacuum their junk drawer? Come on. We always promise ourselves to do something about it but never do. But isn't it odd that when you pay someone else to upend that same drawer and they suggest you toss this or that, it's easy to say, "Yeah, let it go" and wonder why it's there in the first place?

The inhabitants of modern-day digs are walking junk drawers and ruins themselves, in many cases, and can tell you all about it — if you're empathetic enough. Just listen. You have to have a special fondness for humanity in all its various shades of grey. What most people desperately want is a sounding board. They also want to see their lives through another pair of eyes. It makes for an interesting dynamic. Clients may think their heads told them to call, but really, it was their hearts. Simple questions, like "What's that there for?" lead to bigger questions in life, like "How many pencils are too many?" or "Is this the worst you've seen?"

There is a desperate need, among my clients, to find peace and reconnection. What we really need to do is slow down the wheel of life so we can at least make it squeak a tune we like. Gandhi once said something like "There's more to life than increasing its speed." There's no better place to rediscover ourselves than in our digs, chez nous, and no better tool for maximizing the enjoyment of reinvention than Domestic Archaeology.

Choose Your Battles

I get people to choose their decluttering battles carefully. If they let go of too much too soon, they may find themselves hitting an emotional wall. The initial purge starts with obvious stuff. The clothes that don't fit (and never will) can find a home somewhere else before they are relegated to a box in the basement to moulder and supply cozy apartments for mice. There are heaps of magazines with articles you meant to read back in the eighties but didn't. Wedged under the stairs, there are boxes of old records, video tapes, and cassettes, that no one will ever be able to play again, let alone sell. I'm not talking about marketable fifties jazz vinyl, eighties rock, or even something nicely obscure by Robert Crumb and the Cheap Suit Serenaders. I'm talking about the dog-eared, mildewed, Englebert Humperdink LPs, accordion covers of Beatles songs, "Speak Spanish" language albums, hopelessly scratched Sesame Street or Disney 45s that you promised to save for the grandkids if they came along, the clanking box of 1980s VHS tapes the man of the house kept hanging on to because it was once a prized collection. I'm also talking about those brown plastic holders filled with cassettes that were rewound with BIC pens so many times that the stretched loops inside have formed dreadlocks and the little white pad the tape ran across is black and unhinged. Useless.

Then there are the plastic bags so brittle that they feather apart like dandelion fluff. In the rafters, there's that set of cross country skis no one has strapped onto their feet since 1994, and in the back of the top shelf, in a cocoon swirl of sheeting and twine, is your grandmother's harvest gold or avocado green yogurt maker and fondue set that dates from 1971. They're next to the yellowed bread maker and the nested Christmas tins (all rusted), some of which are still sporting wax paper that encased, Paleolithic cookies — all "perfectly good." But none of it is good, really — is it? It's easy to convince yourself that everything is useful and needed. Here's my big question of the day: When does your home cease to be a home and become a warehouse of useful things instead?

Be free from the broken Etch-A-Sketch your grandkids will never use, even though you loved it once, and the bulbous furniture you inherited that would only suit a Byzantine bordello. Get rid of the unplugged, bottom- heavy fridge from 1968 with the packet of baloney calcified in the crisper, and even the old oil tank that dates from back in the days when Pontius was a junior pilot. Recycle what you can, but for heaven's sake, get rid of it all; donate and recycle anything and everything you can, junk the rest. Stop waving aside that vague odour of damp rising from that threadbare area rug or ancient, somebody-will-want-it single mattress slam folded up in the Kafkaesque metal torture device cot you once allocated to visiting relatives you didn't like. Above all, give yourself permission to live without the emotional grip of all that clutter.

Many of my clients imagine family guilt into things. They imagine a parent is looking down on them and expressing disappointment that a couch they once loved to lounge on is being dumped. It doesn't matter how much the cat peed on it or how mouse-chewed it has become; it's a symbol of family, and a treasure. It sounds silly reading it in print, but these are real emotions that hold people back. We'll talk a good deal more about what letting go does for clearing up and buying time for one's future life in my follow-up book — tentatively titled *Stories from the Home Zone*. You want to carve chunks of that time now. Plan the use of your future time to see how much of it is being consumed by the effort of keeping track of junk that doesn't serve you.

Therapy often lies in the acceptance of getting rid of the insulation of "stuff" and moving to a new stage in life. It's hard to have a relative stranger guide you to letting go of things that were part of your life, even someone like a professional organizer, who is looking after your best interests. After all, what do we know of your life? Probably more than you can imagine. So, I play bon cop/bad cop. Not everyone is ready for the shift. It takes some clients longer than others, so now and then, we organizers must be resigned to the maxim "Everything in its time. Everyone in their time."

New Normals

People live in their "Normals," layers of ritual and life that have accumulated over a period of time, dust and all. We absorb tradition and call it our own. We inherit stuff and feel obliged to guard it forever until it's time to pass it on. But kids don't want it. They don't polish silver or display china cups any longer. So, the stuff stays packed away. By extension, people don't have buffets or hutches any more, and these things are no longer anywhere near paid value. Try and sell one on Kijiji sometime and you'll see how people bargain you down to pocket change and then want it delivered.

Normal is a state people are used to and don't question: they do their grocery shopping in the same order every week and keep the layout of a room's furniture, even though it never worked. There are mountains of newspapers tucked behind the couch and mouldering boxes of files from decades-old defunct businesses, sitting in dim basement corners, waiting to be shredded. There are textbooks from glory days at college and cookbooks that no longer play a role in family gatherings, sitting atop ancient metal cabinets like Celtic monuments. Often, people just can't make the effort to get it all gone because letting go of such reminders leaves them hollow. There's an inexplicable inability to label the disposal of their things with a satisfying emotion — to create a new normal that's better than the one they have. Now, they foster only regret.

Of course, there is a sufficiency of clothing nobody wears cramming the inside edge of every closet and filling every ancient box beneath the stairs. The list is as unlimited and varied as human nature. And each item has a steadfast advocate for letting it remain right where it is.

Most people don't believe that their stuff has the power to freeze them into inexplicable inaction until the day they need to get rid of some of it. Only then do they realize it's clutter laden with emotion. Letting go of some stuff requires a grieving process. It may take time. It may never happen.

Most of my clients claim to crave simplicity, and they mourn the lost "best years of their lives," especially when their family was young. It terrifies them to let go of anything associated with those years — the rickety, paint-splintering high chairs, the mouldy camping gear the children once loved, and even, as in one case, a dusty box of unused baby diapers for a daughter now in her forties. I offer people a new set of eyes and perspectives and, more importantly, a new normal. I impel them to question why something is the way it is and force them to ask if there is a better normal. I don't let them put something down with a dismissive wave and say, "Oh I'll decide on that later; that, too, and that, and that, and that." I see the strain of change in their eyes. It is physically painful to face even the simplest alteration. The more life went off the rails, the harder it is for them to accept. I find that if I give somebody that new normal to try on for size, something better than what they've got now, and it works, it amazes them to the point where they ask why they didn't do that sooner. They glow with their new determination. They're hungry for help. Of course, maintaining it all, endeavouring not to slide back into old habits of not putting things away, and tossing useless stuff, is another thing entirely. Patterns are ingrained and hard to overwrite. Life is in the trying.

My pragmatic science-minded brother, Peter, would probably say, "Kinetic energy is manifest" or something like that. He can talk the talk. His world at NASA is moons away from mine, and the stuff he does with Mars rovers and comet probes makes me wonder if mom and dad didn't rescue me out of a litter of sea monkeys.

Organizers step in to serve up small answers that collectively result in big solutions.

We politely confirm the wayward state of a person's environment and gently suggest a course of action that would make them accountable without having to plow through a book of psychology, two feet thick.

What I Do Is Who I Am

When I reveal what I do for a living, I reveal a part of my soul. It took a lot of years to get comfortable with that daily exposure, as I am a shy kind of dude. You wouldn't know that if you saw me fling myself up in front of crowds to lecture extemporaneously for an hour or two. That's another Stephen. I don't know where he comes from. He untucks himself from my back pocket, and he has a grand time sharing stories like the ones I've included in this book — stories and confessions. Confessions you ask? You betcha. We're chock full of them here. This is not your average how-to-get-organized book. If you're looking for keen ways to organize your clothes closet by season, size, and colour, forget it. This is more a peek into our common humanity and my passion for it. It's not so much about our stuff as it is about how we choose to move forward, past, around, and over that stuff.

Organizers will, from time to time, trade their best stories like baseball cards (no actual names of course). It helps reinforce the fact that we share a common bond, a unique profession with very similar experiences and war stories. I do stray from time to time, my train of thought leaving the station like a monologist off on a grand verbal detour, but I promise to eventually circle back on track, so stay with me.

Some of the solutions, motivations, and ideas I've included in this book are ones other organizers might have also developed while on their journey, and these professionals can be forgiven for thinking they are uniquely theirs. There are 5,000 professional organizers in the US and about 600 in Canada. We've all been hard at this for oodles of time now and we've all come up with a lot of the same approaches. Many of us have written books and articles, and posted blogs and hours of videos. My focus is on revealing an organizer's world and how their clients' stories can help a reader adapt an approach that may help them. The trick is adapting an approach to fit the myriad little foibles, levels of energy, life experiences, and ingrained habits people may have.

Clients and organizers alike often have eccentric solutions with which I may violently agree or wholeheartedly pooh-pooh. No one should lay claim to any of them because we've all stumbled upon ways of dealing with the core problem: clutter. The key is how you tell the tale. That and being flexible. I say, read everybody and glean a cross section of common sense from each book you stumble across. But for heaven's sake, make it fun to read, or what's the point? My approach slips serious advice under the radar. Books about organizing seem to have supplanted vitamin books when it comes to giving wellness advice. But there are few organizing books that tell the stories — the human face behind clutter and how the clients have, in turn, changed the organizer. I see those ones stay on bookshelves long after the *Here Are 10 Ways to Declutter Your Closet* books get donated to charity, never having been cracked.

Organizers also find that telling a client how another client fared trying the same thing is hugely useful. It makes clients feel less alone. I don't purloin ideas. I give credit where credit is due if I hear something that works. Like any good organizer, I adapt what I learned in the field and accept that sometimes another organizer has an angle I haven't tried. We learn from each other and always sharpen our skills, freely asking each other the all-important question: "And then what did you do?"

Give me real-life stories any day — even ones that make me cry. Yes, I am a sap. I feel connected to people when I hear them cry. It's unabashedly human. Laughing and crying are the best indicators that you have made a connection. Where there is a connection, there is motivation and forward momentum.

The stories included here are real, embellished only by words and my relentless imagination. They are all my stories, my experiences, things that have happened to me in the tackling of more than 1,200 houses over fifteen years. It's all about how I got into this business and why I stayed so long. (How I got here so fast, I'll never know.) Some situations have cropped up for me repeatedly, so if you see one you think is yours, don't kvetch with litigious embarrassment; you may simply not be alone in your clutter-battle journey. I have nothing but respect for each and every client and realtor I have helped.

I have a rare job where I am invited to dig through layers of other people's lives, unearthing interesting prehistory, the odd shame, and the even odder treasure. I've enjoyed wonderful moments of misty-eyed delight while helping people rediscover who they once were.

It's the kick-starter moment to the journey toward reclaiming their dear former selves. It's a neat process of reinvention, if not reincarnation, and it's really what lies at the heart of Domestic Archaeology.

Part Two: Spring, the Vernal Equinox of Life

To find out how I got into this business is to know something about new beginnings. Nothing shouts new beginnings like my favourite season, spring.

Spring in the northern latitudes is filled with a sudden pleasantness. It's heralded by a collective unpuckering, when, all at once, people sense that the last bit of *brrrr* has been unceremoniously ushered out the door. A sweet mildness descends, and it's followed by an awareness that the equinoctial days are as long as the tepid nights.

While March is filled with more tricks than a clown's pocket, April, ah, April, has hope. It may toss a slush-ball in our face, just to be pesky, but at least we have hope. We know the odds are on our side. Weeks earlier, we cranked the clocks forward like impatient time travellers praying we could also rush the thaw. When spring shows up in earnest, we set aside any dirty suspicions of winter's trickery, depopulate the car of war-weary ice scrapers, bag the snow tires, unclench our arthritic grips from our lapels, and preen for the sun like ambulatory solar panels. Unfettered by head wrappings and snotcicles, we are aware of 360-degree vistas. When the alarm clock stutters us awake each morning, we linger horizontal that wee bit longer just to listen to the sweet clatter of birdsong.

Signs of reawakening abound. Neighbours appear like squinting moles to tip-toe squelch into their backyards to pluck errant newspapers from bushes or unshroud the patio furniture and the sleeping barbecue. They squeak open windows, desperate to let their daughter's poor choice in music out or replenish the air supply in the mouldy vacuum that is their son's room.

More than anything else, thoughts of renewal and reinvention invade our spring craniums. The expression "spring forward" fills the air with possibility that a new, better journey is about to begin or that projects stalled may yet become projects achieved.

I Smell Burnt Toast

This bit is about how I burned out from my old world as a corporate executive. When my "better journey" came about, it was accompanied by an electric epiphany. I had reached an impasse in my life, and the wall I hit was not uncommon for anyone who has endured a successful stint in the wrong career or an unsuccessful one in the right one. I am going to tell you about how I hit that wall in that wrong career and why I had to leave it or simply die. Then I am going to tell you all about the remarkable role serendipity played to reignite my life and carve out my own meaningful right career.

My face plant occurred during a restructuring, while I was working as a senior project manager at a high-profile media corporation. Spring had come, and the latest attempt at cost-savings-disguised-as-improvement was being rigged out and waiting for managerial wind to blow it into full sail. The theme of the year was outsourcing. This usually meant finding the most productive employees, tagging them as redundant, and trading them in for more disposable, less costly, wide-eyed personnel on contract. In my case, it meant being found redundant, let go, then found to be very much needed after all and rehired to do the same job but in a contract position and for less pay. Is it any wonder a steady stream of people burn out of the corporate world each year and search for something else to give their lives meaning? Personally, I think letting go of hardworking, specially-trained, dedicated folks before their time is a form of shameful disloyalty that causes a lasting sense of PTUSD (post-traumatic unemployment stress disorder). Mentoring should be the norm to ease out the old and sharpen the new recruits.

I see it all the time in men and women in their forties, fifties, and sixties who have an eagerness to keep giving but feel jaded and cut short by modern corporate ruthlessness and a lack of compassionate business ethics and foresight. It's a form of burnout I call "corporate de rigueur mortis."

Multi-Multi-Tasking

Being rehired to do the same job often means being asked to multi-task the workload of several recently dismissed co-workers. To me, multi-tasking means doing two things half as well. Multi-tasking is a recipe for disaster no matter how you rechristen it. You miss details, details that matter. There's no spellcheck for that. In my case, work piled on, and, being a conscientious guy, I began taking on too many late nights and not following the general trend of vacating the office and one's mind after six o'clock.

When you are padding away on a gerbil wheel, all you think is that you are moving forward so you must be making progress. Like Pink Floyd sang, I was playing a lead role in a cage.

To make matters worse, I was unsuited to the world in which I found myself, and had been for more than a decade. Though my brother, Peter, had inherited my father's love of and aptitude for science, engineering, and mathematics, I, most definitely, had not. I was cursed with a playful, artistic mind. Early on, my father had wished me well but had earnestly opined that art and writing were "hobbies" a person indulged in, secretly, after a day of real work. He felt any artistically bent choices would only set me adrift, honing a talent for unbillable hours. It's funny how small words can derail and sabotage you in such large ways, especially when some of them are true.

Small Words Reverberate Large

So instead of veering into creative worlds I would have adored pursuing, I towed the line and began a life of cramming my brain with all the things I found physically painful to absorb, like engineering formulas, mathematical equations, functions, calculus, algorithms, and statistics.

Then I played the blend-in game. Nobody notices how miserable you are if you wear a tie. I also took extra classes to make up science credits, and then took them again when I forgot everything I had learned. My brain on science and math was like quicksand, sucking it all in but giving nothing back in return except oatmeal and bubbles. Luckily for me, engineering often required someone with creative spatial and illustrative skills to bring concepts to life. Enter my love for illustration and a talent for AutoCAD.

Ironically, I was hired into the engineering world, beating out dozens of other candidates, because I was good at drawing and spoke French. On the minus side, it suckered me deeply down the road of the wrong career. Year after year, I let it pass as it paid the bills. The career even brought my wife and I to a new city, Toronto. I was accepted in a new job, all the while feeling like a fraud. The people around me wanted to be there, had deliberately trained to be there, and loved their career choices. I never did.

I'm Tired of This Game — Let's Play Another

A wise woman I once married (OK, I've been married only once, and her name is Irene) has an abundance of pithy phrases that are both apt and timely. One of my favourites is "I'm tired of this game — let's play another." This is usually in the context of some aspect of life that has lost its lustre, and it usually involves a job. Certainly, when you aren't doing what you should be doing with your life, using your true talents and making your heart sing, then sooner or later, life will rear up and dump a humongous cow flop on your head. It took me years to realize this and even longer to know that escape was an option.

When you are in your thirties, you can lose a few years without too much fuss, but when you are in your forties or fifties and skyward, losing time is like losing a shoe. It's noticeable, especially when you are in a hurry.

Eventually, you may have to disappoint others to achieve what is best for you, even if you aren't 100 per cent sure of the outcome. Women, mothers especially, would sooner lose an appendage than disappoint family. All you know is that no matter what, you have to stop what isn't working and play another game.

Sometimes it takes drastic steps to start anew. It takes disassociating oneself from the familiar to dive into the unknown. What do I know about this aspect of Domestic Archaeology — the recovering of who you should be? If you'll indulge me to get personal for a bit, I'll tell you about it.

We Are Delicate Machines

The years leapt by as they are apt to do, and I found myself in my forties and working on my own special breakdown. I unwisely worked straight through way too many nights, catnapping with my head on my desk to the dull hum of fluorescent lights. I would snort awake in the morning with the cold realization that my short nap at 3:00 a.m. hadn't worked out so well.

One morning when my wife was dropping off a clean shirt and a toothbrush, I awoke to the worry in her eyes. We were in no position to cut and run. She had left a tenured job at a high-profile university in Montréal to follow my transfer to a city that was new to both of us, a city continually adding new lanes to every road and highway to heighten the mad pace. Now things were going kablooey, and I was becoming visibly unglued. I'd come to the end of the road without seeing it coming; I'd never burned out before: when something goes south, denial keeps you ignoring the inevitable until it steps up and rearranges your dental plan, and you smell burnt toast.

Listen, for all our bravado, we are delicate machines. When we take on too much, make too many decisions, pile on too many pressing deadlines and multi-task, something's gotta give. Do twenty things at once, and you have what happened to me: zzzzzzzt with a wisp of blue smoke.

One defining morning, I found myself standing in the corridor adrift, confused and utterly bumfuzzled. I thought the lights were faulty and flickering, but it was my eyes. I was also many pounds heavier than I am now, thanks to a lifestyle devoid of exercise and punctuated by the tendency to gobble down food court meals between panic attacks. This can play silly buggers with your blood flow.

I thought I heard something go sizzle and zzzzizzle and zzzap! Worst of all, I found I couldn't move forward or backward. I was freeze-frame frozen in place. It terrified me, and I didn't know what was happening. The corridor took on that stretch-to-infinity-movie-camera perspective and seemed suddenly endless. Then it hit me that, in this place, at this moment in time, I was getting farther and farther away from who I wanted to be in life, and if I took one more step, I was going to die, simply die. The thought had a life of its own with a ferocious focus. It was, as I said, a cataleptic epiphany. So, I froze like a statue. A colleague of mine came across me standing stock-still and staring into space with what he later called hollow, stricken eyes. He would later go on to have his own forced walkabout in life and would end up in Mexico raising rabbits.

"Are you OK Steve?" he prodded, genuinely worried. "John," I stammered, "I … I … I … I … I … zzt, zzt, zzt. I quit."

The moment I heard the words come out of my mouth, I knew it was right. I sighed as if I had been holding my breath for days. It didn't matter that I had no other job in the wings. A slab the size of Portugal slid from my shoulders. My friend listened as I babbled, nodding wordlessly. Anyone else would have thought it was time to rent me a seat on the magic rubber bus.

I didn't know what I was going to do or how I was going to make it, but I knew for a certainty that I had crossed a bridge: I was done with my "wrong profession" forever and all time. Casting off the yoke of other people's expectations is beyond liberating. The first thing I needed was a reversal of thinking — to bust out of the joyless job routines that stole my individuality. If your job is not who you are, you are missing out on something special in life. This was the mindset I had to embrace when it came to reinventing my life.

I went back to the drawing board to figure out my skillset. Nothing is lost, as they say, and along the way I had acquired a number of talents: people skills (bolstered by a wry sense of humour that could breech even the most formidable outer wall of the toughest customer), organizational skills, and a hardiness that allowed me to get a job done. The key to transition is figuring out how to use existing skills in an entirely different field. I had to think about what I had always been good at, what made me truly happy. If I did that, I only needed to match a solid desire out there with what I had to offer and to figure out how I could apply myself to it. Now, if only somebody would pay me for it. It was a very big "if only."

Don't Burn the Bridge – You May Need the Lumber Later On.

I've always admired the skill with which drivers of large rigs could back up a seemingly impossible length of truck and maneuver it into a slim alley between buildings, and always, it seems, under the pressure of some impatient moron honking his dribbling disapproval. I could never do that.

Mark Twain once wrote, "We're all ignorant, just about different things." It took me years to admit to myself that I had never been good at a lot of the things I had spent years working at, even though I dearly wished I could be. I confess I am a terrible bureaucrat. Spreadsheets and budgetary forecasts not so much befuddle me, as bore me to tears. Engineering had not quite been a career that had sung to me like a siren's song. It did, however, with subtle peer pressure, family expectation, and the promise of benefits, lure me onwards onto the rocks of my bad outcome.

In hindsight, I wish I had gone another route and changed my travel plans. I think a lot about choices and what-ifs. No doubt, that's probably why, as I grow older, I have an increasing fondness for time travel movies.

Dipping, as I do now, into other lives, I have found a shared commonality. That sense of "what if" is always hovering about in dark corners. When we are younger we just don't think about time and how very fast it takes us for a ride. Rarely do I run into someone doing what they truly love. They do what they can learn to like. It's like an arranged marriage of inconvenience. You follow what will pay a living. It is a cold reality, the letting go of dreams, and our modern society delivers it like the sobering air of a winter's morning. That is sad.

Changing professions late in life can be like stepping into an alternate universe filled with unknowns. You can adjust to some things. Others you just live with, like a new limp. Many people try to shift their profession, but the unknowns become too much and they drift back toward the known, no matter how miserable it made them. Change is too nerve-racking. The one thing people never brace for with change is change. Like getting out of bed in the morning, you're never ready for it. You just have to trick yourself into starting some place along the way.

I was tired of playing it safe and didn't want to fall into another "uh-oh" imitation of a career. I wanted something tangibly real and uniquely suited to my personal strengths and, let's face it, my quirks.

Spring into the Unexpected Journey

Often, when you begin a new and important journey, you're not aware you're on one. You know what I mean if you've ever jumped into the car to return the yogurt your wife didn't want — a small but necessary task — and then found out the universe had something else planned. Call it your spin at the wheel of destiny, opportunity, whatever. What begins as a simple errand turns into a new plan for your life. Instead of getting to the grocery store, you pass a park where a wellness group is doing tai chi. You pull over to watch and chat, and you love the vibe of trying something new so much that you decide to trade in your patent leather shoes for open-toed sandals and move to Fannie Bay, Australia to become a life coach.

Yogi Berra, the famed baseball coach (no, not the cartoon bear with the picnic basket fetish), once said, "When you come to a fork in the road, take it." Sometimes, you unexpectedly arrive at a metaphorical fork in the road, and you hang a sharp right when you were going to hang a lazy left. Yogi Berra also said, "If you don't know where you are going, you might end up someplace else."

When you find yourself at that someplace else, you know it right away. There is a tangible "something different" in the way the air feels, like you are in two places at once and out-of-phase, out-of-sync, with some established order; it's almost an out-of-body experience. You feel both where you are now and where you would have been normally had things gone according to your usual day. You are suddenly keenly aware of all of the alternate possibilities before you: it's a string theory of choices. You've momentarily thumbed your nose at the gerbil wheel of life, the selling of your precious time for a bag of beans, and chosen instead to take your shoes and socks off and walk on the grass. For one brief moment before the void, the universe feels right. That's the way I felt. Without knowing what I could do, would do, I felt an urgent liberty to try something new. I tell you all this because it's good to know how I tumbled into the profession I am now so fond of.

Serendipity often plays a role in our path in life. So, it was with me when I lamented to a real estate friend about my skill set and wanting to apply it elsewhere. Coincidentally, she had found herself in desperate need for someone to assist her home sales, someone with intelligent people skills, a person with a genuine fondness for detail as well as the physicality to sort out a mess and find a way to get stuff gone. In short, she needed a cross between a mover, a decorator, and a motivational life coach. We have all manner of people filling the gap with those skills — relocation specialists, stagers, and, of course, professional organizers. Fifteen years ago, realtors seemed to be at a loss, having to do almost everything themselves, especially prodding homeowners who were reluctant or simply unable to sufficiently organize their homes as quickly as the agents would have liked. Though she was happy to roll up her sleeves, my realtor friend was frustrated by all the dealing with people and all their history-filled stuff. Almost as an aside, she asked if I would like to take that on. It challenged and intrigued me, something I hadn't felt in a long time. I didn't even know there was a thriving profession called professional organizing that had thousands of members around the world. I just liked the idea of working with real people for a change. That, and there was money involved.

The UP Button and the Hero Mindset

Reinvention makes you dwell on your past and what really made you who you are. One small piece of the puzzle called Stephen Ilott came about when I was a kid. Way back then, I was enthralled with a wonderfully cheesy, action adventure serial called *Rocket Man*. Unlike today's high tech, CGI effects-driven heroes, this was a syndicated black-and-white hold-over from the 1950s, when square-jawed men wore baggy suits and punched each other's hats off. It was a simple delight from a time when a quarter bought you an all-day sucker that turned your mouth various shades of puce.

Rocket Man was a hero who had found his calling and never lost his confidence. I admired him for that. His jetpack was also dead simple and worked on a knob he could dial UP or DOWN. To get flying, he'd dash a few feet, hit his mark on a hidden trampoline behind a papier-mâché desert rock, and flick the dial to UP, then off he'd go into the sky to punch off a few more hats. I later wondered if the makers of Viagra ever thought of using that footage in an ad. Something about that helmet would drive the message home.

Rocket Man had a clear, precise, and methodical career to-do list — use his nose for trouble to follow the rumple-suited minions to the cave of the maniacal death ray scientist, engage in a series of back-and-forth haymaker wallops with said bad guys (over crates of hissing dynamite) until they can't get up again, and save the corn-fed, snarky girl reporter with the wide shoulders and wonky ankle. I admired that. That's what I wanted in a job.

When you do begin to seriously rewrite your own story, a good idea is to adopt that hero mindset. The hero mindset says you think beyond the immediate bill-paying scenario. You need a bigger picture. You need to place yourself where you feel a reconnection to humanity in order to feel alive and a part of the world once more. You need to be a catalyst for good and forward momentum in many lives. You need to be appreciated. More than anything else, you need to be the hero of your own story.

Be off Trajectory on Purpose

Why do we feel so alive and so scared starting something new? Are ruts so comfortable? It's probably why successful vacation packages are designed to make you feel as though you are living another person's life and why soap operas are so popular. Why don't we make that other person us? Trade in stuff you don't need for moments you do. Get lost on purpose.

A few years ago, before cell phone GPS was so widely available, there was a European travel group that had walking tours of Paris and London. Once you were there, they gave you maps to the wrong city to deliberately get you lost as soon as possible. It's in deliberately getting lost that you see things you would never have seen if you had stayed on the path to which everyone else was glued.

I get lost all the time when my wife, Irene, navigates our trips. We look forward to it. They say birds find their way via a magnetic sense that uses tiny amounts of metal in their brains. I can categorically state that my wife doesn't have any metal in her head at all. That's a good thing. The thrill is in the expectation of the unknown. When driving backcountry along the wine routes, we even ask the car where it wants to go. "Car?" we say, and Car listens attentively. "Where do you want to go?" we ask. And Car hangs a right and a left and another right. Before you know it, we arrive at a sweet little vineyard in the middle of nowhere, or the back end of it, a place we've never heard of before that becomes our new favourite destination.

I want you to know that you are not your circumstances; you are more, you are renewable. You can start again, but it may not be the same kind of start you imagine. It's a tougher start, but it can break through walls of your own making. You can be forty. You can be seventy. Forget the years lost. You can look into who you once were at a time you enjoyed being you and reignite that joy again, this time using your true self as a guide. You have to be willing to let go of the things you didn't know were dragging you down.

We are a sorority of sorts, those of us who have survived the wrong profession, the wrong marriage, the wrong house, or simply the wrong life. I was on the hunt for something to bring me back to a simpler kind of business, something creative and honest, a special interactive kind of something that I could both teach and learn from at the same time.

My own heroic self-image was that of a teacher. I never realized how much that was true until I became an organizer. I envied the modest guy with charm, talent, and a pocket full of philosophy, who got along with a few nifty tricks backed by some impressive physical bravado, while all about him, people were losing their hats. I wanted a career like that. To say my family was skeptical of my options is like saying the Elephant Man had a little puffiness around the eyes. But a chance reconnection soon had me turning my UP dial up, sooner than I thought.

Guinea Pigs Can Fly

So, what's all this got to do with either decluttering your house, or my journey, you ask? It's got to do with a rethink of what serves your life and what doesn't. It involves letting go of what is expected of you from family and society. Do you need to have grass as your front lawn in order to fit in, or would you rather have wild flowers? Is the price of being an individual worth it? I had to find out a whole lot about what doesn't serve a person's life, or my own, before I could presume authority status as an organizer. I had to be confronted with new problems and realities. I had to think outside of every box I had ever neatly created. No question, my first clients were my guinea pigs. They didn't know it at the time. From them I built up my experience. Each story I relate in this book speaks to that learning process. Often, I had to rethink my own prejudices about what constitutes a normal house or way of living, in order to step aside and listen to what made my clients happy. Did they truly love having columns of newspapers all over the place and really only wanted a better way to organize them?

I did know that my new world involved learning new things each and every time I picked up the phone and dove into the lives of people wanting change. My first task was to learn how to listen. I thought I knew already. I did not. My instinctive solutions were quite often served up on-the-fly to fill the eager pause of anticipation a client would dangle in the air between us. Some of my ideas stuck about as well as statically charged socks tossed casually on a wall. That is, not very long. When I came up with a particularly good idea, a client would tell me so, and I'd think, "Yeah, it was. I better write that one down." I also learned that there were times when I needed to seriously regroup, such as when I had a client I couldn't help in the least. The biggest lesson at those times was that failure quite often precedes knowledge.

True Fiction

Often, when I tell people about my experiences they say, "Come on. That can't be true." Surely, I must be exaggerating. I think that too many folks live a very singular existence. They travel the same road to work, eat the same meals each night. They don't realize the variations of life happening all around them, getting brief glimpses of off-kilter lives via the unreality of TV. Even then, in the back of their minds, they think, "Yeah but that's TV. It's not real." What is TV but true fiction? It procures out-of-the-norm experiences and peppers them with commonalities we all share to make them approachable; it edits out the dull moments, then uses sleight of hand to manipulate our emotions, with our permission.

The stories clients tell me vary widely, and they tweak my ungoverned curiosity. I love to listen. I love to step into them, and sometimes I am relieved to step out of them. I know what it's like to have to reinvent one's life. Getting paid to guide others to do the same is a treat, although that all depends on the ingredients I have to work with. Some people need a minor tweak while some situations are not as easily salvageable. You can't make lemonade out of potatoes, but you can make a fine sour mash.

My First Lessons: The Calls of the Wild

Those phone calls were the first big challenge in my new profession as a declutterer. They began pretty much the day I alerted the world that I was a home organizer, way back in the spring of my decluttering years. I didn't know how to go about advertising, since people couldn't figure out what I did until after I did it.

I always liked the phrase "hanging out your shingle." It refers, of course, to early doctors ready to face new clients and putting out their sign: "Doctor So-and-So, Saw Bones." Or some such treat. My shingle-hanging moment came when I chose a name for the business. I knew early on, instinctively, that mine was going to be a business of deletion rather than one of addition — decluttering more than organizing. So, it seemed natural to be "Decluttering.ca" — I added the ".ca" as a built-in marketing aid. If anyone forgot my contact information, all they had to do was remember the word "decluttering" and tack on the Canadian ".ca"; then they could find me online any time. It seemed to work.

When you officially murmur to the world the news of your existence, you expect a trickle in reply. My responses began arriving via every form of media: email, telephone, texts, Facebook — any way people could reach out. It's been that way ever since.

I confess, I am still overwhelmed by the surprisingly frank level of emotion people catapulted my way. Each spring, I brace myself for the calls of the wild, the as-yet-faceless strangers who, fuelled by the hope of finally getting organized and starting life anew, hum my cell phone to life across the morning paper. When it all started, I felt somewhat childlike, facing a whole career where people were going to expect me to sort out what they had been living with for years. A friend of mine says I "straighten out people's paper clips." It's a nice metaphor.

I often hear the courageous voices of women on the phone revealing, in hushed whispers, that they dream of turfing their spouse's insufferable junk before he gets back from his golfing holiday, but they would consider a few less clumps of dog hair a victory. It does take courage to open up to a total stranger. Other frazzled men and women have lamented that they couldn't walk a straight line in any room without barking a shin on their significant other's latest hobby monument. One despairing man slid into Bollywood dance steps every time he entered a room because of his wife's chaotic, ever-present piles of magazines. Another person called simply because she liked my face and felt I was the right person at the right time to move her life forward. It didn't matter that I was a hundred miles away. Yet another individual emailed me hoping I would help her via Skype, as she was a full continent and two time zones away. I did — help her that is.

Some exasperated souls explore the idea of setting something up for a sister or mother and expect me to break the wonderful news that help is at their door. No pressure.

Two different husbands called one spring to tell me that their wives were going to be out all day and that I had to drive over right away and throw out all of their stuff, money no object. They were at a loss to understand why I would refuse such an easy gig. I, on the other hand, had a hard time not imagining the whacking great kafuffle, if not vociferous divorce proceedings, that would follow — ARROOOOGA, ARRRROOOOOOGA, DIVE, DIVE!!!

Often, people ask me to come by and tell them what to throw out or donate. They simply don't have a clue how to do it.

Many believe a professional organizer has the inside track on how to get top dollar for their "valuable collectibles," — collections of Beanie Babies, Cabbage Patch dolls, crystal unicorns, vintage Easter Island toothpick holders, or stainless nickel Bavarian spoons.

Then there are calls, like the one from the gruff, insistent woman who made the concerted effort to inform me she was completely and utterly organized and didn't need my services in the least, thank you very much. I have no idea who she was. I never heard from her again.

I'm a Realtor — Info Me Up

Real estate agents can be the funniest callers. They are one part cool customer, two parts frenetic circus master. My best and most difficult allies are real estate agents. They are the single best referral tool for an organizer, yet one of the hardest to reach with traditional marketing. I often feel like Jeff Goldbloom in the original *Jurassic Park* film, waving road flares to get their attention. But when they need what you can do, know you can do it, and expect nothing less than for you to do it yesterday, then the phones never stop until they get you. Many homeowners need the services an organizer provides and almost none of them are willing to pay for that service. This is particularly true of men.

The realtors who hire me on a regular basis know to lay out all the facts with as few surprises as possible. It's an earned courtesy. However, now and then, realtors, anxious to list in the spring market, ring me up with an imperiled panic and, worried I may turn them down, hedge their bets by sugar-coating the task ahead or talking quickly, in a hypnotic voice, in order to seal the deal before I can refuse. I call that "the treatment." The voice on the line is tentative and probing but matter-of-fact and insistent that they need me ASAP. Funny how the acronym ASAP — As Soon As Possible — has come to mean absolutely immediately, and the "possible" part has been lost in translation.

The majority of realtors are succinct in what they need and when they want it. And most of the jobs I am asked to do are mercifully doable, even though sufficient time in which to do them is usually non-existent. That's fine. I kind of like the panic jobs. I get to bare my teeth and dive in, and anything I can get done is a pressure release for all concerned, especially the realtor.

I have a stager friend, who I truly adore, who sometimes tries to slip in some "treatment" hoping I don't pick it up. Whenever she uses the term "eezee peezee" I cringe, waiting for the other shoe to drop, wondering what sciatica-inducing hell I am in for.

It's a slippery thing. The jobs sound doable at first but quickly reveal themselves to be hugely not doable. Ever. Here is a slightly exaggerated example…

Realtor:

> "Hi. Jean Luc at Patisserie D'or gave me your name. You know — that bakery with the great tarts — anyway, I have a difficult client on the fourteenth floor of a split-level condo high-rise without parking

access. You'll have to risk a parking ticket at the mall down the street. Be careful. I hear they tow. The building you want isn't numbered, but it's the third of four. Or is it the fourth of three? Anyway, there's only one service elevator, which hasn't worked in a few months, and the building manager makes my teeth itch. She guards the place with her life — not a pleasant person. She has issues and barks. I swear she barks. I need you to remove a Wurlitzer pipe organ by tomorrow so my flooring guy can replace the living room carpet and put down some Berber for the showing. It has stains, lots of them. The carpet, not the pipe organ. They have dogs. You may need to take the organ apart but it's solid. Just don't damage it. You're insured, right? Do you have tools? Quiet ones? Call one of your metal guys. They do it for free, right? Let's do that. You can't make noise — condo rules and, well, you-know-who. You need to book the service elevator ASAP, if it's working. Good luck. (Snort laughs.) It's only available Tuesdays. What's today — Thursday? Anyway, donate the organ. Sell it; I don't care. The family doesn't know she's giving it away, so expect some resistance. She has a difficult forty-something son. He may be there, on the couch, playing video games on the big screen in the living room. Oh, yeah, we have to move that, too, and the couch. They both weigh a ton. The couch is all old metal inside, very spiky and pinchy. Watch your fingers. The son sleeps in the living room. It smells like he does, anyway. He can't help move anything, anyway. He has a bad back. Give him a coffee coupon or something to get him out of the place. Or you'll have to tell him. I understand you do this sort of thing. I heard diplomacy is your thing. Oh yes, I told my client you would defer your fee until closing, no more than three months max. She's good for the money. Best get her lawyer to send you something in writing. I would. (Laughs again.) He's out of town — the lawyer. Hawaii, I think. Figures. Do you have a truck? I hope you are OK with large dogs? I do mean large. Did I mention the dogs? Are you insured, personally, I mean? They're not house-trained. I don't think the son is either. Are you allergic to mould or mice? Oh yeah, I forgot about the rabbits. Don't leave the door open."

You get the idea. OK, I kid. A bit. Whenever a realtor runs into some bizarre, undoable job, usually involving getting rid of cast iron daybeds or pianos, they seem to become that one person with my name on the tip of their tongue. I seem to be that guy at the end of the sentence "I know a guy who knows a guy." You know in movies when they say, "Send in the 'asset'"? Well, I've become the asset.

I'm not alone. My wife gets that too. Whenever we're walking down the street some place, total strangers walk right up to her and ask her for directions. It's like she's wearing a pinwheel hat and sandwich board announcing that she's the information lady. There could be a thousand people milling about in the street, and the aimless ones will gravitate to her like she is magnetizing Styrofoam peanuts.

Do we carry an aura — we doers and keepers of the secret flame? Maybe I deserve to be "that guy" for pulling a rabbit out of my hat a few too many times.

Often realtors look for someone else to own a vexing problem. Often knowing that guy who knows a guy can mean the difference between nabbing a listing or wasting a week. It's a tough business, with heaps riding on good faith and hope.

Realtors, eager to get stuff gone, also text me terse overtures, such as *How much?* They fail to offer any further insights about the job, just *How much?* Are they talking about a two-room condo filled with dust bunnies or an 8,000-square-foot McMansion filled with collectible ceramic giraffes? Do the clients have dogs that bite? Do they have children who bite? Do they need garbage bags or dumpsters? Do they also want to donate things or get info on selling all that in-demand bone china, silver plate, and crystal they can't believe nobody wants? Am I working with someone young or older, someone with ADHD or OCD, or worse — a hoarder? Who knows? One thing's for sure: they get annoyed when I respond with *How long is a piece of string?*

Now and then, young realtors will text me expecting an instant response that very nanosecond, and they are unable to comprehend the delay. Technology has robbed many people of simple patience. It can be both disconcerting and amusing at the same time when they then insert their own assessment of what went wrong. (I confess that often I … wait for it … do not carry my cell phone on a job. It can get smooshed really fast.)

At the end of one long day with a client, I read the increasingly judgmental texts from one such young woman. The realtor began her nervous barrage with *Need quote.* It was followed a couple of minutes later by *Text me now*, then *Call me*, then *Call now. With client waiting.* Her phone message ran a similar line and was followed by another text: *Left message. No answer.* Finally, I was given the bum's rush and a curt assessment of my business acumen: *Unprofessional, not impressed.* It was like the evolution of an entire relationship had run its course in the span of a few moments without me ever being present. Time and real estate wait for no man or woman.

Opportunivores

Another special kind of hazardous person to which we in the modern world are subjected with increasing frequency are what I call the "Opportunivores." (A perfect expression, not original to me, but one I wholly adopted.) Realtors and organizers alike have to watch out for these lovelies. Opportunivores are the folks who will use your talents mercilessly, your time guiltlessly, and your energy and enthusiasm without recompense, all the while calling it an opportunity for you. They are the rapacious ones who are very adept at getting ahead, especially at someone else's expense. You may know one or two or three of this type of person, the kind who doesn't so much make friends as cultivate acquaintances for future use. Some are thrown into the role by circumstance and economics, while others are born to it. More than anything, an awareness of how they operate sharpens your ability to detect who to avoid if you want to stay in business.

Once you have that antennae tuned, their antics can be quite instructive. You need to start by focusing your Mark 1 Eyeball keenly on Opportunivores to pick up the subtle hints of danger. Recent studies of dogs and how they watch a human face can give you a clue here. We used to think dogs watched only the eyes or only the mouth (looking for the baring of teeth, for example). But dogs have an instinctive "whole face" strategy. To get along, they have learned not to trust a smile. In the dog world, baring one's teeth is a sign of aggression. In the human world, it has become a tool of deception. Dogs have learned to zero in on the eyes, then look back to the mouth to see if the signals each is sending actually does, in fact, match the other. Computer programs count the rapidity of this shift, then catalogue the dog's response: placation, or backing away, or, in some cases, bracing for attack. With Opportunivores, you must always brace for attack. Always trust the eyes — truly windows into the soul and the window into what an Opportunivore has in mind. Paying attention to the verbal element and how someone emphasizes their words enhances my ability to detect something not quite right and prepares me for the moment that is preceded by the words "Oh, by the way…"

I know I am whining here. But confess I must. I have to confess to you, oh reader, about all the stuff that gets turfed my way, to give you the full sense of what it is to be an organizer.

Some Opportunivores want free staging and decor advice — lots of it. Many callers, not letting me get a word in edgewise, have kept me on the phone while they walked from room to room to room and, describing what they see in detail, want to know how I would solve the problem.

In the early days, I allowed this random intrusion, feeling it was somehow my duty to my fellow man or woman. I also wanted to get the word out about organizing as a profession. But I found the I-just-need-to-get-your-opinion questions soon became drawn-out speed-dial ones about life and the meaning of existence. No mention of things like "I was about to step out of the tub" would deter them. The phone would ring at 11:30 at night and my wife would rouse on one elbow with an eye squinted shut like a boxer on a bad day and mutter, "Who the hell is calling at this time of night?"

Some Opportunivores became well known to us, and we organizers would warn others to beware because what they wanted was to pick your brain clean and move on without hiring anyone. For that reason, few good organizers do free consultations unless it's either a sure thing or a service for a frequent-use realtor. Like most things these days, the spoilers made it necessary to set some new rules. Those errant calls showed me that a number of people truly felt entitled to great gobs of my time and effort — at no cost to themselves — in the grand quest to solve their clutter problems. Even social services agencies referred their most destitute clients my way at one point, noting that the individual had no money but needed to be decluttered right away or they risked eviction. I quickly made it clear that I was not a clutter prevention hotline or social service charity. I give back in so many other ways and frequently do more hours than I charge for — for members of my favourite demographic, at least: seniors. The free therapy calls have thankfully stopped. The calls for pro bono decluttering have not, and I get one every few weeks. I love cultivating good therapists for just that reason, and I freely recommend them to those who need one. Who knows, I may need one myself someday.

A few Opportunivores, with far fewer scruples than average, feign poverty after an entire day or two of work has been completed. The standard pantomime involves patting their chest pockets and noting dismissively that they can't find their chequebook, or they painfully lament that things have been tight lately and they can't afford to pay after all.

No contracts signed or assurances in advance make the slightest difference. One clever woman got a whole day of organizing out of me, paid, and then called her lawyer to tell him I had been called in to teach her computer skills but that all I had done was move stuff around. He did as his client requested and leaned on me until I returned her cheque. I also once packed up a storage trailer POD and house for a long-time trusted client for a move to the United States. The client miraculously vanished leaving the thousand-dollar invoice unpaid and never returned any communications. Funny how the incentive to pay for a service is somewhat diminished after having received it, especially when the service provider, taking it in the shorts, has little power to do anything about it. It's often simply not worth the hassle, legal or otherwise, for them to pursue the matter.

Some Opportunivores offer to trade their stuff for my time, usually stuff they were decluttering anyway, like god-awful bulbous furniture; or ginormous, two-ton TVs; or past best-before date vitamins they can't sell. Or worse, they want to barter for services I can't use, like horse whispering or psychic-graphology. If, to be charitable, I agree to a trade, the value of their object skyrockets, and suddenly I am working ten hours to earn a prized milk bucket now valued at $400.

There seems to be no limit to the downloading people think they can get away with while making their problem the purview of someone else.

The best one I can remember was the case of a fellow who asked me to sell his priceless life-sized wax Madame Tussaud statue of John Lennon. Since he was in immediate need of cash, he suggested eBay. He wanted a minimum of $10,000 for it, preferably in hand-delivered cash. He had attentively repaired the hands and redone the hair to vintage specs. My guess was that he lived alone. When I asked him why he didn't sell it himself, he begged off, hemming and hawing, and finally confessing that he had borrowed hefty money from loan sharks to buy it, then skipped town. I thought, yeah right, how many wax figures of John Lennon are out there and how quickly would I find a couple of unsavoury dudes darkening my door grunting, "We don't know where dis guy is so we're gonna take your car. Dat OK witchu pal?" I declined the fellow's kind offer to share in the ready profits and "opportunity."

You have to know when to say nuh-uh to Opportunivores.

You learn to gauge each and every client by their potential to pay. You just have to trust your gut. Thankfully, along the way, I have not only learned life lessons from Opportunivores but also developed an ability to spot the danger signs of an impending bad client. That's when I give the nod to colleagues who are blinded by the need to nab a new client and who seem oblivious to the risk ... or who even hope, with gnashing teeth, that things will turn out OK, despite the obvious warning signs of trauma to come. It is a talent honed from cold experience that no quickie course can ever teach you.

On one consultation, a friend who is a hugely talented stager and renovation expert brought me in to do my usual preliminary review of a home before she could work her miracles. In the driveway, after we had met to figure out what would need to be done, I shocked her by stating that I had a bad feeling about the job, and I deferred. She was surprised that I felt my gut was telling me something I could not put into words. It may have been the punched in TV screens, I can't say, but my gut said run away. Later she was impressed and wondered how I had known there were going to be challenges on the job. She had run into costly problems with the client. The gut never lies.

Smitten Detectives

There is something keenly offbeat about the tangled situations people tell me about. They pique my curiosity even if they make me want to grind my teeth searching for solutions. Organizers are like mystery-smitten detectives who can't help trying to sort out other people's lives, whether they want us to or not. It is one thing we share, no matter how diverse the background that has hurled us into the profession. Organizers love to be the ones who unleash the Phoenix, rather than the Kraken.

Since I specialize in decluttering, I love to discover when and how stuff took over to the extent that the family home became hostile territory. One woman who got my attention was so frightened to go into her basement that she noted with true trepidation, "Oh no, nobody goes down there. We hear things." Now that's something I have just got to investigate.

The lady, a senior with mobility concerns, didn't descend into the basement much, in any case. I don't think any family or friend had either, not in quite a few years. Many such homes are called "heritage houses," and at one time or another, housed founding families of the community — some of them respected. These places are found in the unlikeliest of urban settings, hemmed in by modern starter castles and convenience store malls. Life was rough and tough in the early days, and quite often, some family member had died in or around the home under curious or horrible circumstances. Such stories usually crop up unbidden, if you're around long enough and encourage the telling. All that, of course, contributes to the overall air of creepiness one feels making one's way into the depths of such old places, where early construction methods are on full display — no nice drywall coverings to hide imperfections. The stone walls of this lady's house had shattered masonry with the odd patch of mould and a glistening of damp. Overall, a deep, abiding mustiness filled the air, along with a fine scent of powdered concrete and the occasional acidic whiff of unidentifiable liquids in bottles whose labels had long since tattered away. Dark, thick beams of wood, inches above my head, deadened sound as I ducked low beneath them. It was a full-height basement and not a crawl space. It's just that people in the old days, even up to the 1920s, were remarkably shorter than they are now. The history books seldom talk about height. Many of the floorboards above bristled with rows of ancient, flat nails protruding down like upended hedgehogs offering to cleave the scalp of the unwary. This house, like many I have been in, had crumbling floors and edged troughs for water drainage, making for uneasy navigation. I couldn't help but stop and stare in wonder at the unruly knots of knob-and-tube electricals hanging indifferently above one such trench cut into the floor. How the place had made it into the twenty-first century was a wonder in itself. The basement had a section of wall cracked and crumbled away, displaying pure earth — I marvelled that a river hadn't decided to run through it. The ancient furnace hadn't been replaced in decades, and dripping pipes and other waterworks added to the odour of time laying on everything. It's curious that so many owners of such abodes are surprised that the possessions packed haphazardly in such long-untended areas are worse for wear.

It was clear that the various noises spoken of were from the huge variety of items that generations of mice had regularly scampered over at one time or another, but mostly, the cast iron furnace rasping its last puff of usefulness. It's funny how common sense about the origin of strange noises goes flitting out the window the second one of the few light sources suddenly buzzes and flickers out, leaving you standing in deep shadows. Stillness surrounds you and, at those moments, you remember the tales told to you of the original owner who froze solid one night out and made it back home, possibly, as a ghost, to lament from the depths of the basement.

Like in any house I declutter, this was a matter of hauling up the debris, displaying it for the owner, and assessing its usefulness, one mystery at a time. Once brought up into the light, all stuff becomes treasure or trash — usually trash to divert to someone else to love.

Careful Sifting

It takes careful sifting to find the clients who make my vocation choice a joy rather than an exercise in futility that makes me want to fall limply to the floor at the end of the day like a pile of clothes. Admittedly, I choose my clients much as I did when I first haltingly muttered to people that I was an organizer. I take them on more readily if they are aware that they have a problem and are actively involved in restoring things to the perpendicular. I also need to know who owns the problem. If a wife owns the problem created by her oblivious husband then he has to be involved in the solution. If not, nothing is going to change. My job is not to change him if he doesn't invite change.

Can I Ask You — On a Scale of One to Ten...

At some point every client needs to know how they measure up clutter-wise: "On a scale of one to ten, how do I rate?" They grimace, waiting for my reply like I am about to hit them with a plank. They are much relieved when they know I have seen far worse. There is hope in their eyes. Hope I can work with. Hope, like spring, grows on you.

Lessons About Patience from a Rocky Start

I learned early on to cultivate patience for people who were testy and impatient even before we started. Methodical organization is too time-consuming for them. They often ask, "How long is this going to take?" as if they had a parking meter about to expire. They suck their teeth in incredulous disgust at my assertion that it may take a few visits, or that it might be inconvenient. One woman, who had a devastating hoarding problem, dismissed my assessment that it would take many months of hard work by noting another organizer had assured her it would all be handled quickly in a couple of weeks. The woman was sleeping on the dusty couch in her family room; the upstairs bedrooms were practically cut off because the stairs were unpassable and mounded with teetering piles of "essential" garbage. That was two years ago. I am sure she and the promising organizer parted ways in short order, leaving the hoarding woman still searching for someone else to tell her what she wanted to hear, namely that it could instantly be made perfect, without effort. Charlatans swear there is such a thing as instant results and they prop up unrealistic expectations. Fortunately, nothing surfaces faster in this business than a reassuring lie. The market is also flooded with amateur "declutterers." Everyone is a declutterer. Few of them really know what it means, or how much work it really requires, physically, mentally, and financially. Some "organizers," as I have learned, are even allergic to dust or terrified of insects and mice. Others, to my amazement, simply don't like people. Go figure.

I also have to compete with the less-than-scrupulous people who are posing as organizers. One woman, who hesitatingly brought me in to her home, was a super nice senior with mobility issues. She had let a sweet-tongued couple in to organize, and they had proceeded to isolate her and renovate what didn't need renovating; they then created inukshuks out of her possessions, and did nothing more. Many thousands of dollars later, she was no closer to having her linen closet organized, which was what she had originally set out to accomplish. Not only that, but the flimflammers she had hired took items, such as her fridge, for themselves and repeatedly showed up wearing the clothes they had "decluttered" on previous visits. As the old poem goes, "Sweetest tongue has sharpest tooth."

Nothing grinds my giblets more than someone taking advantage of a senior. It should be a capital offence. I can only hope that what goes around comes around for those tricksters. It was a big PR job to restore that lady's faith in organizers.

Be careful of sweet fast-talkers who tell you they can declutter you quick and easy. I suggest you tell them, "You're on probation for four hours — go to it."

Find and pay for a true professional — someone with experience. Get a plan and an estimate as best you can. Sure, it can cost a fair chunk of change. But, as they say, if you think working with a professional is expensive, try working with an amateur. An honest professional offers the real deal. There's no push-button way to get around the nitpicky, one-thing-at-a-time nature of decluttering your life. Think wee bits. The only way to avoid having to face a huge mess all at once is to do it a little bit at a time. It's called maintenance. Alas, too many people are surprisingly hands-off about who owns a problem and how it got that way. Lie to yourself all you want; the stuff will still be there when you're done being frazzled by it.

Absence Makes the Heart Grow Flounder

I wonder about homeowners who ask me if they need to be there at all when I declutter their homes. I have received phone calls to make sure I am on route, only to be told that my client can't actually be there themselves. I can never figure out what they're thinking. Now and then, I arrive to read notes taped to mailboxes or front doors: "The keys are in the mailbox. Do what you have to do, and be sure to lock up when you go."

Early on, I would go inside and do what I could do, only to get the inevitable sour late-night call complaining that I moved stuff around, or worse, the dirty implication that things are missing, which they later find anyway. Nobody ever apologizes, ever. You take it on the chin.

Some clients watch TV or answer emails the whole time I am there and are visibly distressed when I have to interrupt them for input about their stuff. I almost feel the need to text them to get their attention during the session. These escape mechanisms are often apparent in the first few minutes. Deferred decisions are followed by the preferred method of running away from that decision. More often than not, the cell phone (with its array of apps, emails, texts, etc.) is to blame. So much importance has been placed on instantly maintaining the connection and the soothing reinforcement of self, that the cell phone has become the new "glass teat" (a term used by sci-fi writer Harlan Ellison to describe TV). It's the perfect "run-to" device for clients who are stressed about having to make a real decision and not a deferred one. Questions such as "What do you want to do with this item?" provoke responses like "Ummm ... wait, I have to answer this email." So it goes, with the next item and the next. I have had to become downright bad cop, unpleasant with some of my young hired assistants, who have a very hard time refraining from texting and answering emails while we work together. One young lady I had hired for the day not only refused to turn off her cell phone while working but also repeatedly texted her boyfriend in front of a visibly annoyed client. She thought it would be a good solution to go outside "for a smoke" whenever her texting need arose, making it all right, in her mind, despite my warnings to the contrary. She was proven wrong when I dumped her bag at her feet and urged her on to further employment elsewhere, much to her astonishment. Lesson learned for the next job, maybe.

The Game's the Thing

Many clients and their family members absolutely have to have a TV blaring, some in multiple unoccupied rooms. Boys favour video games for hours on end, mostly the incessant tactical-shooter variety, which offers complete and total shutdown ("I just gotta finish this level!"). The teenage son of one client, already four ear-piercing hours into a shooter video game filled with sirens, tactical team walkie-talkie squawking, urgent music beats, and high-powered gunfire noises, lost all reason when I attempted to declutter around him. His parents were preparing the home for next-day photography and subsequent listing on the market. There was no time left for mucking about. He wailed like an epileptic banshee, insisting that he had to finish his level with the assembled tactical team. The team were all teens of similar age, one would assume, connected online. He stomped and screamed uncontrollably for his mom to kick me out while he lost all his reason and civility.

Gaming advocates quote convenient findings that shooter games improve both vision and the ability to discern many objects at once. If the many objects at once are people fleeing your gun sights, is that a wise thing? Weekly events around the world speak volumes about violence and its origins in popular culture. The most-attended movies each summer are ones with scenes of anarchy and those that reign supreme with mass destruction of whole cities. Audiences are in awe of the spectacle. Name a recent superhero or action film that didn't have hundreds of random victims fall among shattered buildings. The most-watched shows on TV involve frequent instances of graphic murder. And this is vicarious entertainment. But when the real thing plays across our news screens from Paris or an American grade school in some tiny hamlet we are shocked to our core. How can this possibly have happened? Kind of an odd dichotomy, isn't it? Playing video games (note the word playing) for hours on end, every day, is an addiction. Being screamed at by an out-of-control teen (who was asked politely to stop playing a game so important things could be resolved) has nothing to recommend it. But again, as the declutterer, it's not your house, so you have to step back.

In my job, I see things, commonalities. Our accepted forms of entertainment should perhaps be rethought, if we are to mature as a civilization. To me, most video gaming is humanity thumb twiddling on a massive scale. It is big business softening the edges of accountability and maturation for profit. There are games and there is learning. One thought to parents is to be aware of what your children are learning via the games they play. And not just children. I have met too many wives whose thirty- or forty-something husbands stay up late or get up early before work to play games. Is it a good use of their lives or their time that could otherwise be devoted to family? I watched too much TV as a teenager. Those are hours I'll never see again, and I regret not talking with my parents more when I could have. When technology tugs on clients during an organizing session, it heralds my imminent departure as much as when husbands start rattling keys or the loose change in their pocket. "Here's your hat. What's your hurry?"

Wouldn't it be nice if a popular trend was crowdsourcing ideas to solve world problems — a massive ongoing mind database that would give people the same kick as watching something "blow up real good?"

This is not the first time pop culture and TV entertainment norms have gotten in the way of realistic expectations around getting stuff done. I find that home-and-garden shows have a lot to answer for when people think they can get heaps accomplished in the blink of an eye — just like on TV.

Lessons on Overthink

One example was a client who burdened herself with overthink and left no real time for the actual doing. I learned about ladies hobbling themselves with overthinking and overtasking early in my career. This one woman brought me in for a two-hour session that was scheduled to start at 9:00 a.m. When I rang the doorbell at 9:00 a.m., she swooshed the door open and glared at me. Beginning a working relationship with the client already mad is lovely, right? Instead of "hello" or "hi there," she just said, "I wanted to start working at nine." That confused me for a moment, like someone had tilted a Luxo lamp into my eyes to wring out my secret rocket formula. I said, "Um, I'm here and ready to work." I looked at my watch. "It's nine on the nose, CBC time," I chirped brightly. She repeated her initial opener exactly as before, as if I hadn't heard it the first time. "I wanted to start working at nine." She led me into the kitchen and showed me her schedule board. "See that?" she said. I did, and said so. She immediately announced that she had to pick up her children from soccer practice at precisely 11:00, so we had to do the kitchen by 10:00 and dining room by 10:30. Already, I could see she had shaved the session down to ninety minutes. She felt this could be easily achieved and had thought it all out, even though she had previously been unable to do any of it alone. I quickly found out why. She had carefully followed the TV shows, making note of all of their methods. When I deviated from the TV method she told me so. "No, that won't work. They do it this way on TV, and a lot faster," and so on. It impressed her that the organizers on TV made a quick and tidy job of the whole house in one half-hour episode. She was perfectly aware that TV time and real time were not the same, but at the same time, those were standards to which we should apply ourselves. She had everything planned except the "doing." It was penned in on the fridge, our session's agenda, all very neatly printed out with time frames:

9:00–9:15 Upper kitchen cupboards

9:15–9:30 Lower kitchen cupboards

9:30–10:00 Children's play area

10:00 Dining room, buffet, hutch, bookshelves, etc.

My client became visibly annoyed when I pointed out that she hadn't scheduled time for the unexpected, nor had she allotted the actual time it took to physically sort, assess, and deal with things. Worse, with hellos and review of the space and expectations, it was already almost 9:10, and the upper cupboards had not even begun to be addressed. It was ridiculous. Her hands rose up, palms facing each other, as if squeezing an unseen yoga ball. She then raised them higher to beside her head. "How can I schedule the unexpected if it's unexpected?" she huffed. I tried to explain what I meant, but she was already super stressed out.

    The funny thing about overplanning is that the planning takes up a lot of the energy that should go into the actual doing. More often than not, as I explain a plan of action, I am already quietly putting it into action, in order to grease the wheels of progress. Before they know it, something is visibly accomplished, taking the edge off the expectation and anxiety of where and how to start. My client wanted to know my detailed plan (if hers was so unreasonable), something I could not give her without seeing what she had to work on. This meant opening doors and having a look. Without realizing it, I had become an adversary on her turf, pushing my hidden, unwanted agenda rather than performing exactly like the TV ally she thought she had scheduled. She was having none of it. When I actually tried to deal with the clutter item by item, pulling things out of the overpacked cupboards, she panicked, decrying the piles of things I was suddenly forcing her to consider. Any effort or suggestion fell under scrutiny and was immediately dismissed. My client began waving her hands about wildly, palms out like Liza Minnelli doing a jazz dance. I was frankly taken aback. Only when I shovelled things out of sight once more and closed the doors, did the hands lower and the voice become calmer.

This universe of mine had tossed an unknown quantity right in my face. My only avenue was total compliance. The front door beckoned to me. I asked her to show me how decluttering was to be done, if not by methodical means. She took this overture as an attempt at sarcasm. Breathing deeply in great gulps, and with nothing accomplished in her imaginary schedule, she lost all semblance of civility and began to visibly unravel. It is one of the worst fears of anyone who works with the public, the sudden cold smack of realization that the person you are dealing with is not entirely stitched together and may need some form of assistance more profound than what you can offer. That moment can be as startling as it is educational. You are out of your league and dipping into the domain of therapists. It also makes you feel like you're treading water in a shark tank. You are tempted to turn on some recording device, just in case, as backup. It speaks volumes about the need for anyone dealing with the public to have some basic training in human psychology.

One thing is for sure, you immediately want nothing more than to extricate yourself from the situation. As much as I honestly desired to help, nothing was going to work. The whole session had been doomed by my client's unrealistic expectations, combined with whatever it was that was already stressing her life to the point of unravelling. It left me no choice but to back away carefully, as if from a lit cherry bomb, and offer to find her a more compatible organizer. I left, charging nothing for the attempt, feeling deflated. That must be what office temps feel when they get to walk away from a particularly unpalatable job placement while seeing the trapped eyes of despair left behind as the elevator doors close.

It was the worst half hour of my young career, to that point. More would top that visit in the years to come. Stay tuned.

Those kinds of clients taught me to study psychology big time. One has to define expectations, real or imagined. I now ask people to tell me what they think will happen, what will change, and what they expect me to bring to the table; most of all, I now recognize the importance of a preliminary consultation, by phone or in person, whenever possible. Although the vast majority of doors you walk through present pleasant challenges, now and then you step into quicksand, or worse.

If a consultation begins with any kind of impatience on a client's part, I know my efforts will be less than stellar, in their eyes and mine. The impatient ones know just how it should be done, and they are not shy about telling you so. The fact that their way has been a dismal failure eludes them. They know what they want: instant solutions, and they want them NOW!

Many people unrealistically expect huge amounts of decluttering to get done in the time they've allotted, or what's the point of trying? This results in an all-or-nothing mindset. With no planning for what ends up being many hours of focused attention, and no effort to build interim steps in along the way, the "nothing" option prevails, time and again.

One of my clients maintained an office piled with paper because she didn't have a label gun and absolutely needed the files to have perfect tabs. I needed her to see that she was enabling an internal limiting force that could be overcome only by actively inserting interim steps into her day. This would move her out of the morass of doing nothing. I suggested Post-it notes until she could buy the label gun. You can't get to your second floor without climbing steps. Can you instantly read a book you have only just picked up? Nope. You go page by page and gladly grow by the methodical read. Paper teaches patience.

Parallel Normals

Expecting help and advice is one thing; being open to advice and admitting there is a problematic habit worth changing, is another. Some of my clients have what I like to call Parallel Normals (PNs). Their viewpoint seems like something from another reality, and they seem oblivious to either cause and effect or the need to change. Their normal isn't what I call normal, so I have to readjust my view of the world in order to be able to sort out a solution for them. Here are three examples:

Shoes

One potential client called me in for a consultation to discuss the fact that her shoes, purses, and clothes were taking over the bedroom, living room, hall closet, bathroom hutch, and finally, the upper kitchen cupboards in her apartment. Clearly, she had a shopping habit beyond what her space and finances permitted. The purchase was all. Unopened bags were everywhere, their tags still attached and dangling like ornaments that pirouetted slowly in the breeze from a slightly opened patio door. There are so many people like this now that TV shows are overflowing with the subject. Again, a psychological element reared its head. Here was a level of clutter that had been born of various social and psychological needs to satisfy either the perception of feeling part of a higher snack bracket, or simply the attraction of the endless array of beautiful things that this client could own, now, on credit. There were elements in the situation that were beyond my scope at the time, and I suggested as much. As to the actual organizing issue, I suggested additional shelving, an extra enclosed storage unit like an armoire, and even a bigger apartment. I stressed the importance of getting rid of some less loved items to make room for the things she truly loved, and I suggested that this lady might want to cut down on new purchases. That old chestnut philosophy of "take one old item out when a new item comes in" rarely works. I suggested relocating some items to bins in the building's locker storage area. The client didn't like any of these ideas and took umbrage at the suggestion that there was an accumulation problem here of her making. Clearly, I hadn't understood her lifestyle needs and her simple request to make it all work. She also pointed out that she had spent valuable time, now wasted, in searching me out, and I had failed her miserably. Our encounter ended with my client telling me that she needed to think about the situation for a few months, as a client had invited her to

Hong Kong, and she now had a perfect opportunity to buy some shoes.

I confess I almost ended my new career before it had begun. I thought that if all the clients were like this one, I simply couldn't go on. I despaired at the prospect. Thankfully, many more clients arrived who were level-headed, agreeable, and willing to change, and they really wanted an ally like me.

My early experiences taught me that I had to stick to the issue of organizing and offer solutions as best I could, unless my clients expressly asked, "How did I get this way?" In general, I left extreme therapy to the therapists. As time went on, I became more comfortable with people and more curious about the hows and whys of their clutter. My growing arsenal of ideas became invaluable.

Dust

Another case of a parallel-normal viewpoint came with a client who called me in to (a) help her with a dust issue, and (b) reorganize everything we could in two hours — which was the limitation of her budget. The past-its-prime brown brick apartment building in which she lived was one of those tomb-like edifices where every footstep on the polished granite echoed endlessly. It was the kind of building with a laughably highfalutin name like The Ravenscragmoor Building or The So-and-So Towers. Most of these buildings would be more appropriately called Toad Hall.

Steeped in institutional greens and greys, the dingy walls of the dim hallway closed in on me, and stale cigarette smoke drifted from beneath apartment doors. I wanted to push the shaky elevator floor buttons with my knuckle.

The lady's door buzzer stung my ears. I heard someone wrestling with a metal slide chain. When the door tugged open about halfway, my client smiled sweetly around it and beckoned me in. She noted that I would have to make my way over some things in the hall. The "some things" in my way were significant enough that I had to half-climb, half-high-step my way along, all the while balancing carefully like a Wallenda balancing on a high wire over some dangerous abyss, hugging organizational supplies close to my chest. It was an obstacle course reminiscent of the Japanese game show *Most Extreme Elimination Challenge*. I half expected to be walloped by a geyser burst of water or a giant papier-mâché fist if I misstepped. I slid into the living room to be greeted diffidently by the lady's significant other who declined to get up from his comfy threadbare recliner. Instead, he rose up on one cheek to grouse that "her" dust was affecting his health. For emphasis, he added a gurgling, smoke-filled cough that nearly dislodged a chunk of grey lung, as well as the long ash dangling from his cigarette.

The dust was copious in places, so much so that it seemed like freshly fallen factory soot when backlit by the sunlight streaming through the holes in the curtains. The lady was at a loss to understand where it all came from. I didn't want to get into the fact that dust is made up of everything from old bits of skin to retired meteorites. Everything produces dust, and it's all just part of the decaying world around us. The key is to habitually scoop it up and put it someplace else, defiantly preventing it from smothering your abode. It requires a device to help you, like a vacuum cleaner, say.

I felt for her plight. Poverty is a loop. Its despair can wear you low. Everything costs money and effort. Nevertheless, this lady was bright, likable, hopeful, and pleasant, and I was happy to do what I could to enlighten her during that one and only visit.

My client's significant other also noted that she had thrown away her jewellery because she had said it was broken. What valuables she had kept were almost worthless, including the ubiquitous Beanie Babies that she, like everyone else I know who owns some, doggedly assumed would fund her retirement. As for the jewellery, I think she had misread an ad similar to ones I see every now and then that make me laugh. They read simply "Sell us your broken gold." You gotta love that — "broken gold." I can almost hear the fly-by-night huckster wheezing, "Sorry lady, I can't pay you top dollar for dat ring 'cause it's got broken gold."

My advice: If you have gold or jewellery to sell, seek out reputable buyers and jewellers. They are fair and they exist. They'll tell you the going rate for stuff. Most of it is going to be melted down anyway, including coins, flatware, and jewellery. Collectible value isn't what it used to be. Forget sentiment. It's all about the metal.

In the end, after two hours, I was able to bring about a small measure of nice to the lady's life. I moved the couple's master bedroom to a "guest" room that had far more space, something they hadn't considered. Nobody stayed in the guest room, as the couple never had guests. They didn't own a vacuum cleaner so I suggested they buy one, or a Swiffer, perhaps. In the meantime, I couldn't do much about the dust save whisk up the larger tumbleweeds: sweeping in a space with sealed windows was not a good idea.

The work I did for this client represented a small victory that gave me the energy to keep going for the next client, and the next.

I have since done sessions at homes with dust layered so deep it made the home look like a surreal scene from an artsy movie. In one home, it was layered so thick that it reminded me of the American South where they have a weed called kudzu that blankets the countryside. I remember driving past an abandoned farm that had been reclaimed by the weedy stuff, and I could just make out the eerie outline of a barn and tractor beneath it all. I was glad I didn't see the outline of the farmer as well, planted in mid-stance and buried in foliage. How Stephen King-ish would that have been?

At one home, I wiped the TV screen clean of a remarkable amount of brown nicotine-tinted dust that rippled like muddy snow on a windshield. (Again, people think I am kidding.) I had assumed the owners didn't watch that set, but I was wrong. They marvelled at the sudden and miraculously crisp image I conjured up for them as though it were magic.

In another home, the dust was so bad that the dog pacing restlessly around us grumbled and sneezed constantly. "Grrrr ... mumble ... shhhhkkkkkew! Grrrr ... mumble ... shhhhkkkkkew," he rattled. I knew the dog's ears also itched because now and then he would lower his head to the floor and repeatedly paw at them. More often than not, pets snort-sneeze to expel foreign bodies from their irritated noses — things like dust, pollen, and chemicals. It says something about the air quality in your home. Listen to them. Be a pet whisperer.

Honestly, everything attracts dust. Make regular cleaning the norm, especially around electronics (like computers) and in the winter, when your house is sealed up (especially if you've stretched sheets of plastic drum tight on all the windows). The plastic prevents air infiltration. I even get people to vacuum their walls and ceilings. If dust collects on the desktops, don't you think your walls have layers of it too? Have you ever vacuumed your walls? I doubt it. Also, get a good air purifier. They work wonders. Change your furnace filter all the time. I could go on.

Until you have experienced a house where the inhabitants do almost nothing in the way of cleaning, you will likely dismiss outright what I am saying. It is a PN you just can't fathom. Organizers and social workers know otherwise.

Nowadays, I try not to dwell too much beforehand on what I am about to walk into. I just go and experience it. It took some time for me to get to that point — to trust in my abilities to riff, cajole, and ad lib organizing solutions on the fly. It was running into clients like the dust people that helped me develop my I'll-see-when-I-get-there philosophy. I am not there to judge, simply to be an ally in people's efforts to move forward.

I confess it still befuddles me when an otherwise normal client calls me in to solve a problem but then takes offence when I suggest a change in the habit that created the problem in the first place.

Stuffed Toys

One such ongoing habit expressed itself in the form of cuddly stuffed toys that fulfilled one woman's desire to add a little character to outings with her daughter. It had been a harmless enough habit at first, but I could see it had blossomed into an expectation on the part of the child that I feared would rear its head in later life.

It was a cute little game: when my client and her daughter went out shopping together, they also had to find and buy the girl a stuffed toy. All good and well until this resulted in an overpopulated basement that looked like the stuffed toys had, like rabbits left to their own devices, taken over. There was also the issue of the child's feeling of resentment when an outing did not result in the opportunity for a toy. The mother had made the mistake of asking the child's permission to delete possessions to free up some space. Clearly this strategy hadn't worked. I pointed out to her that perhaps, just maybe, she was conditioning her daughter to subconsciously need to purchase something every time she went out in the future. This was a later-life-problem-in-the-making if I ever saw one, the kind where you go out for a carton of milk and come home with another Louis Vuitton handbag instead.

As with the shoe lady, the act of buying can come from the need to have attention paid or from a feeling of guilt or inadequacy. Fear and guilt are the tough culprits. People beat themselves up over all manner of perceived shortcomings. Without deeper introspection, it is almost impossible to discern motivations. One thing for sure — this mother hadn't considered that in order to fix the problem, it may have been necessary for her to tweak her own habits. So instead of changing habits and deleting ritual buying, she opted to add shelves. At least this offered the chance to create a rotating toy archive and discretely eliminate a few items over time. Using vertical spaces was a short-term solution, but I reasoned that sooner or later "out of sight" could mean that a few of the fuzzy blighters could be snuck out the door.

Poke Some Holes

Not all stuffed toy collectors look at their collections in quite the same way. One client I took on when I was much greener taught me to listen carefully to how people talk about their inanimate pets and their parallel-normal ways of thinking. The woman had a number of stuffed teddy bears. While my assistant worked diligently, packing another area of the house for the lady's upcoming move, I began clearing her office, and I dropped a dozen teddy bears into plastic garbage bags and moved them out of harm's way into the hall. At one point, the lady stopped, drew in a breath of panic, and asked where I had put her little friends. When I showed her, she cried out in horror that they were all suffocating. She then frantically poked air holes in the bags. My assistant, hearing the kafuffle, came running. We exchanged subtle glances as if to say "Ooooookay, altered reality!"

To this day, I never assume anyone's reality matches my own. Everybody has a coping mechanism that serves them very well. If it keeps everyone vertical and paying taxes, it's all good. Who's to say that my coping mechanism isn't just as strange? What I did learn from this client was the importance of letting every client know what I am doing with their stuff, each step of the way.

Be at the Helm of Change So You Can Enjoy It When It Happens

By now, I was well and fully into my new profession. I had encountered an array of people who all shared a common ailment: clutter. They all, more or less, longed for change, and they were ready to embrace it. I loved leading the charge and going along for the ride. I confess I am never happier than when the bad-vibe clients blip off my radar to make room for the kind of people I really love to work with. Fortunately, those ones have become more common as time goes on. They are the spring-forward-minded clients who want to move ahead, who want to be involved, who want to reinvent their lives, who want to see how it's done, and who know it's going to take time, patience, and effort but who are game as heck — and could they start today, please? Love 'em!

But back in the springtime of my decluttering career, I was just beginning to catch a glimpse of my missing and elusive purpose. Was it my passion, after all, to be the catalyst embedded into other people's lives?

Can Daddy Move Us to a Neat House?

One spring morning, such an opportunity came in the form of an email that intrigued me. I was impressed by the number of exclamation marks the young mother reaching out for help had chosen to use. It sounded dire. *Young family needs your help!!!!!!* We all have our tilting point, our own intangible, but keenly felt, brink. There was no mention of it in her email, in fact there was nothing included other than the mysterious subject line, so I was curious.

When I knocked on the door for the consultation, it wedged open just a crack. Once more, a shy, pleasant bit of a face tilted into view, replete with apologetic eyes. People always apologize for the state of their home. It tells you they are aware that things are off. They urgently need an opinion on just how off they are and what can be done about it. People want options when the problem is options — too many directions and too many things to which to apply said options. People escape behind options.

The woman behind the door said, "You have to push a bit to make a path. We don't normally come in through the front. We use the kitchen door in back." Similar to my trek through the dust lady's apartment, I found myself shouldering the door and carving a path through the uneven piles of stuff everywhere. I was the first non-family visitor to the home in two years. I had told my client not to clean up since I needed to see how she normally lived. She had complied.

Isn't it amazing how clean our own houses get when we expect company? Don't we rate that level of clean all the time? It's also funny how we make sure to wear our glasses when we clean for impending company.

It was clear that this lady had lost herself in the pace of trying to keep up with and care for her three children, one of whom clung to her like a koala and yanked her hair down to one side, making it look as though she had a stiff neck. It gave the lady an inquisitive look. Two more gamins raced about, steeplechasing over obstacles. The expectation of being the perfect mother for the perfect family often grinds a woman downhill, unless help from her husband, extended family, and friends arrives to assist with the order of things. Without that support, things can get pretty scruffy. A woman has to make choices.

I noticed that this lady was so drained by doing it all alone that she seemed to be hanging in the air like an aging Macy's Day balloon. Her eyes drooped and her speech was slow. At one point her son, aching for attention, pulled a bag of flour from the basement shelf and dumped it all over his head. She simply moaned in tiny wasp breaths, "No … don't do that," while the boy coughed and grinned.

Not everyone is prepared for the role of stay-at-home caregiver. The focus, 24/7, is on family. Keeping up a house and a marriage most definitely requires a partner to share, daily, in the execution of household tasks. The barrage of laundry alone can back up and bury a couple. I see a woeful lack of laundry maturity in the houses I visit. There are few things that contribute more to the creeping dankness of a home than smelly old piles of clothes. The shock of surprise young wives display when it dawns on them that this is all their problem is fascinating.

Young women often lament that their husbands simply drop all of their clothes and towels and smelly sports bags and food and anything else droppable on the floor and never, ever, pick up after themselves. These downcast wives then beg me for solutions to the problem. I confess I have few ideas other than giving the sloppy culprits a place to drop their junk. In all honesty, I cannot change people's behaviour if they themselves don't want to change. The ladies often find this attitude in a professed professional organizer unacceptable, and they regard this as a failure on my part, rather than something outside of my jurisdiction and more in the domain of family counselling.

In this particular home, loose objects from every imaginable corner of the house covered the floors, stairs, and surfaces. The dining room table was buried. The living room contained paint cans, computer wires, toys, and paper. Dirty laundry, including underwear, was everywhere, and the stairs were a trip hazard of this and that. The kitchen was piled with dishes. The garage was piled so high with things that I had to climb in to assess it properly.

After seeing it all, I asked the lady what had prompted her make the call now. It was something her little daughter had said, she explained. The girl had asked her, "Can daddy move us to a neat house?" It suddenly became clear to her that the disorder in the house was having a detrimental effect on her family. A mother or father will put up with a lot of mess for themselves, but when they see that it is having adverse effects on their children, it shakes them into action. Personal embarrassment is no longer an issue. Protecting the children is paramount. One would think that this idea would come into play much earlier, but so often it doesn't. I needed to engage in a major excavation project in this house if I was going to help this family rediscover their lives.

I asked if the daughter displayed any signs of messiness outside of the home and my client noted that in school, the teacher had observed that her daughter would just drop her coat on the floor instead of hanging it up.

Be Aware When Things Leave Your Hand

With the young "un-neat" family in need, as with many young families, I saw people who had become so overwhelmed by life's pressures that they rebelled by not doing what was expected of them in an attempt to stop the constancy of it all. Rebellion came in the form of neglecting to put things away. So, the landscape of this family's life became the jumble nobody saw, or was allowed to see.

Soon the new normal had changed to include the dust and mould that wouldn't stop increasing; plants that were knocked over, spilling their dirt on the floor, their tendrils long desiccated into a Tim-Burton-set piece; and spilled glasses of juice that had become art displays with plastic toys stuck to them like flies in amber. I've found endless cups of what must have once been drinkable liquid pushed under beds only to mould over and turn to powder. Some things that are dropped need immediate attention or they become part of the landscape that you breathe in every day. No wonder so many new cases of child asthma appear each year.

Some objects become the tasks people plan to get to when there's time ... but there's never enough time. The tasks make it on to lists, and then the lists get lost, only to be rediscovered in a kitchen drawer months later. This house was like that: a house full of deferred, "get-to-later" moments.

To create a sense of comparison, I used a Hula Hoop to help my client micro-focus. I placed it on the floor and had her focus on and deal with only what was within the circle. It took time to keep her in the loop, so to speak, but it worked on a spot-by-spot basis, and the task of worrying about only that one area seemed to do the trick.

I assured my client that this happens a lot, the drifting of focus. She had put time into the important thing — the children, which was nothing to be ashamed of. But now the mess had intruded on their lives, safety, and psyche. Action was imperative. And now my client had help: me. She needed a small idea that would work big. I had noticed a common problem where people, unable to face dealing with an object, defer any decisions to some vague time in the future. The problem is that every object is dealt with this way until it all becomes one big, sliding pile of deferment, too painful to address. So, they run away from it. First a pile, then a closet, then the room, then the spillover to the whole house. Like anything left untreated, the problem only gets worse. That window of opportunity, the moment of do or don't do, is brief. That's why I ended up calling the solution The Thirty Second Rule.

The Thirty Second Rule

I'm sure other organizers have come up with something like this. As I mentioned, there are a few precious seconds when you pick up any object, be it litter, a pencil, a book, or anything else that is out of place. You want to move it to where it should go. If you hesitate more than a few seconds, however, chances are you'll start thinking of the next thing you have to do, and your attention drifts. What happens? That need to empty your hand is pressing. The item you picked up gets dropped, and it becomes part of the landscape. It also likely now falls into short-term memory space, and good luck remembering where you put it later. You may think, "Where did I put that?" but you more than likely have to go to the area you last saw it in order for your memory to kick in. That's why we end up at the other end of the house looking for something, then, forgetting what we went there for, we have to go back to where we had the thought, to remember what we went off looking for in the first place. The trick is to realize that there's a moment of deferred decision.

The avant-garde performer Laurie Anderson once sang that walking was a form of controlled falling. You fall and catch yourself, and you do it over and over again. In many ways, catching oneself falling into old deferred habits, in that brief moment of time, is like that.

The Thirty Second Rule helps you focus on the object long enough to calm down and get it squared away. It even helps to count aloud. Your brain goes, "Cool, thirty seconds, no rush." Think about teenage boys who grab a drink of juice and then leave the glass on the counter before bolting away like a cat disowning the litter box after use. How long does it take to rinse the glass and put it in the tray of the dishwasher? Count it out sometime. It's amazing how you can, in that thirty seconds, put something where it belongs. So, attack a series of cluttered things like that, one at a time, one after the other, and give each one thirty seconds. See how many items get put away.

We needed to focus on this lady's home on a moment-by-moment basis, so we could slowly get her world back in whack. It's so important to get people over that first hump. When they take the reins, they glide along nicely.

I had to be frank and get the young husband engaged in pitching in more often. His wife needed his help to define each room by use and to remove or relocate what didn't fit. He was willing, thankfully. I detailed a list of potential hazards I saw hiding in plain sight. There was a mouldy area (from water damage) that the children had been playing in. The potential for lost time makes a guy sit up and take notice, so I pointed out to the dad that if his child were to get sick he would have to fit time into his schedule for emergency medical visits. It was a perspective he hadn't previously considered. It worked.

The couple wanted to know what they could do between my visits. I sent them regular emails of the photos I had taken and circled specific objects in them. *See this box*, I'd say. *Tear it up. Put it in the recycling box in the garage and email me when it's done.* Guys keep every box they have ever owned, with the Styrofoam still inside. They rarely use these boxes, but they stubbornly hold onto them.

A few days later, I'd get an email about the boxes or whatever task I had asked the couple to complete. The email would say, *Done, along with this and this. Now what?* And so it went. This process saved them money and gave them a sense of doing a lot themselves. I was invited back unexpectedly, a few months later, and I was astonished to see that the house was immaculate; the wife's demeanour had changed radically. She was beaming, bright, and hopeful, and she and her husband had worked collaboratively on the house issues. It had brought them closer together. They became my poster family-of-the-year. When I arrived at the door, the daughter warned me that I should take off my shoes right away in her mom's new clean house, a point gladly taken.

This was a small but happy triumph, and it put me further along on the road to being the motivator and teacher I wanted to be.

You can see these things easily enough as an outsider. The hard part lies in offering something better than what your client has now, something a whole lot easier to implement, something that sticks. I needed to not only validate this lady's deeply felt emotional need to organize her home but also give her a deep-seated feeling of not just keeping up but moving forward. Once you make that connection, you build on creating the new and better normal.

The Thirty Second Rule and Focus

A sharp-minded guy I know, writer/producer Rick Green (his introduction graces this book), co-founder of TotallyADD.com, has a way of looking at focus that is similar to my own. Being an ADD kind of guy himself, he has spirited insights into the mind and focus. His site is well worth bookmarking for webinars, solid information, and insight. Rick suggests we break focus down into three layers.

The first layer is the thing you are focusing on. You focus on something and, as in my Thirty Second Rule, you have a few precious moments to act and keep acting. Some people who live with ADD hyperfocus on a task to the exclusion of all else; they can also hyperfocus on sports, almost self-medicating on adrenaline to get the same level of feeling some people get from a much less passionate level of effort. This can either hobble a person or allow them to excel at one thing.

The second layer of focus relates to how long you are focusing on something. This dream-like moment is evanescent and has you potentially looking off into the distance in a short period of time since, all too soon, your mind starts focusing on other things.

The third and most important aspect of focus, then, is being aware of the moment when your focus shifts off into the ether. Be alert to that moment. When it happens, be aware again of the tangible quality of the item in your hand. Feel its weight and importance, and imagine into it the time it needs to travel to where it should go. That moment when your attention is drawn away is key — and you must refocus just long enough to get'er done. Use the Thirty Second Rule then, most of all. Check out Rick's great documentary *ADD and Loving It?!*, which he made with his creative partner Patrick McKenna.

Garage Sale Confidential

Before I head out of spring and into summer, I need to get one last big pet peeve off my chest — it is a tradition that takes place just before summer spreads its warm embrace: an execrable event that occurs each and every year, in almost every neighbourhood. It's something I call Garage Sale Confidential.

Something about May and June disgorges a home's "left for later" chores. Spring has signalled change and flags are flying full mast. After a winter of sprinting precariously between car and house, May has us hauling open the garage doors, standing hand to chin, and wondering where to start. April is too early for that task, and we're all still too comfortable with the words "Go away, I want to sleep."

Something about May gives us hope. Maybe it's a feeling of time ahead, time at last. We yank hoses clear of their wobbly moorings, undock lawn mowers from behind bags of environment-friendly salt-like ice-melting product, and take stock of the accumulation of things we no longer need, or never did. We even surprise ourselves by what is disgorged from the shadows. Along with the requisite solid bag of cement comes a cheap hose so stiff it looks like a giant dusty loop of licorice, a netless hockey net, two 1980s-era aluminum lawn chairs with terminally frayed seat straps, a clutch of wicker Easter baskets with the oversize handles that nobody loved but you, and a lone punctured soccer ball. There is a framed, disco-fonted poster of the New York skyline with cracked glass and mildewed matting; a neatly kept box of burned-out fluorescent tubes; a stack of china plates, packed stiffly with yellowed sports pages; a sky-blue suitcase you remember seeing in a photo of your mom on a trip to Pompano Beach in 1977; an apple juice tin full of rusty nails you meant to straighten out; a wire-frame reindeer with a broken neck wreathed by a string of bulbless lights; an electronics box full of spare parts, remotes for things you no longer own, and instruction manuals from old washers; and, of course, in the loft, the spare door (from two houses ago) that your husband desperately needs.

We take stock of all the detritus and can't help thinking, "Hang on, this stuff is worth a fortune. I'm going to have a garage sale." OK, gents say this more than ladies, but facts are facts: one man's detritus is another man's detritus he can turn a buck on. Nothing inhibits decluttering like almost-found cash. We'll get into the actual value of stuff later, but, for a moment, consider the pluses against the minuses of a garage sale. There aren't many upsides, so one has to savour them. Let's start with a happy plus. You may, if you're lucky, actually make enough for a nice dinner out. Hooray. Add to that the deletion of a whole world of dump droppings and you are all smiles.

Secondly, it gives the kids something to do. If you don't have kids, borrow some. It'll give them something to do. Will they stick with it all day? Not a chance. Kids now exercise the attention span of a flea before they need to bow their heads in reverent praise of their electronics. Before transforming into epileptic moan-bots, however, they may learn valuable interactive communication and bargaining skills that'll serve them well in later life. Plus, they will learn how to make small change. They can also earn their loot the hard way (if you're paying them), in small increments, just like real people. Good real-world training.

Garage sales give you a chance to meet neighbours you normally spy only from a distance. The ones you like, you would know by pair names, such as Bob and Sue, Mitch and Pam, Patrick and Arianna. These days, we talk less and less with the folks with whom we share perimeters and more and more with the people a digital divide away. We have hundreds of friends on Facebook and allow perfectly good real friend material right next door to go uncultivated. A garage sale gives you a chance to catch up. You may also be selling something they may want, bonus.

However, the dip side of a garage sale outweighs the pluses by a country mile. Forgive my snarkiness here, but if you've given a garage sale in the past five years, you'll remember the misery the task invites and nod your head in sad, solemn understanding.

During garage-sale season, my neighbours get keen on having a multi-family street sale. Upon signalling one's public intention to hold a garage sale, a magical, metaphorical barn door yawns agape, unleashing a jostling, entitled menagerie of scowling cheapskates, filchers, and hardcases, all itching for a bargain, if not a freebie or three. Garage-sale bargain hunters are a desperate breed who show up at 6:00 a.m. to pound on your door and demand to see what you've got — and could you hurry it up please, they have a cab waiting. So, in a panic of duress, you drag out the mostly unmarked items two hours before your stated opening time. There already, as well, are eleven venomously competitive people, hopping from foot to foot, impatiently fingering through the now upended boxes, like sniffing, dismissive raccoons. Then, dropping your stuff from pincer-like fingertips like it was soiled laundry, they leave without so much as a tepid, "Thanks, but no thanks." You may get a shrug if you're lucky.

Some stay on, urging you to hurry up and bring out more. Boney fingers jut out. "What's in that box?" they demand. Sniff, sniff. To which you have to shamefully admit you don't know and haven't set everything up yet, or even priced anything. You're apologizing to rude strangers in your driveway. When the diggers find something they like, they inspect it like it was your passport at the border crossing. They also tell you to put your stuff on a table and not the ground. People don't like to bend down.

Then the aggressive bargaining commences, with you on the defensive. Some want a vastly better deal because

1) They drove so far and gas is expensive (as if that should be factored into your asking price).

2) You said there'd be antiques and all they see is this crummy silver plate and some mismatched china cups.

3) They want only a piece of the item, so why should they pay full price? (The standard offer is a take-it-or-leave-it 50 per cent of asking.)

4) You'll never sell the stuff so you might as well give it up for cheap, and "Look, that one is broken. You didn't know it was broken? It is. Look, see there." They'll just do you a favour and take it away for their garden. Then they're off to pour scorn on the next poor sap and nab a resale prize like it was part of *The Amazing Race*. No time for civility.

More than likely, you'll be treated to a petty thief or two. How delightful these miscreants are. Nothing drains the joy out of a garage sale faster than having to confront someone tucking your wife's ceramic doggie statue up their sleeve as cool as you please. Often, these are the same characters who, after inspecting an item clearly marked in huge digits, flutter it at you like they're waving bunting at a sea-bound cruise ship. They petulantly ask, "How much?" When you point out the price, they give you the sourest lemon face in the world, shaking their head from side to side like you've just told them you found the droppings in your cat tray satisfyingly moist. If you refuse to play nice, they dump it down, only to pick it up later when you're otherwise preoccupied, and walk off with it. Tra-la-la-la-la.

My wife once watched in astonishment as a woman with an expensive overcoat draped over her arm slipped item after item under it. She slipped back to her car to drop off the loot then returned, wreathed in smiles, to pilfer anew. I didn't care. The cheap-thrill karma was on her head. You just know if you had YouTubed her blatant act of petty larceny, her lawyer would have eaten you for lunch for damaging her delicate reputation. I wished later that I had removed her hubcaps and offered to trade them back for the stuff she had purloined. That would have been fun. That's the stuff you only think about later, when you're steaming and more courageous.

At a garage sale, you also get the persistent bargainers who agree to the price of an object, pile it all up with the other stuff they've agreed on (out of reach of anyone else) then ask, "Now how much for everything?" It's as if bulk sales suddenly mean big discounts and an instant adjustment in what they already agreed to pay. If you unfairly disagree, they walk away from their mound. They're waiting for you to panic and say, "OK." Don't. I like to watch them walk away, pretend they're not interested, then have to come back and try again, all for something worth $3.

There are the G-salers who give you a fifty dollar bill for a twenty-five cent item and expect change, seeming aghast you won't leap at the chance. These are usually the same dollops of humanity who, when buying something for ten bucks, give you the choice of making change for a fifty or accepting the easy fiver suddenly flapping in your face. I tell them to go look on the floor of their car. Eight out of ten times they magically find the extra change in their pocket. I'd rather tell them to go fetch a stick. That's not bargaining. It's just plain tiresome, and worse, they think they invented the ruse.

You have to establish boundaries; no, they cannot use your bathroom to try something on or get their kid to stop pinching his nether regions and pee. No, they can't duck under the roped-off area of your garage and dig through a few drawers to find a part for something they have at home. No, they can't stick a few items to the side of your house for a few hours while they think about it. No, they can't take the item back to their car where their money was conveniently forgotten. Who forgets to bring money to a garage sale? You also have to draw a line in the sand for people who want to leave you their kids or dogs while they check out the other sales on the street. You also have to circumvent the folks who casually walk their ginormous moose-sized dogs through your displays. The creatures always seem to have bullwhip tails and hip problems. Like epileptic kangaroos, they lumber from side to side, knocking over anything the least bit delicate, then leave trails of drool as thick as oil in their wake.

Some G-salers go too far in denouncing the appalling condition of an item in the hopes of undercutting what they consider the indefensibly outlandish asking price. This is your cue to have fun. Agree wholeheartedly, then brightly smash the thing into pieces in front of them. Nothing lights up both your faces quite as much.

Finally, no you aren't interested in trading for something the G-saler just bought down the street. The neighbour won't take it back? Not your problem. Is it my imagination, or are there a whole lot more con artists around than there used to be? (See Opportunivores.)

When you shut it all down at 3:00 p.m., the neighbours stop by for a regroup. They are ready with a "How'd ya do?" and the "Ah well, not so great." Then you both swear an oath to never hold another garage sale again, ever, and mean it. Next time, you'll just give it all away. This brings me to…

The Outdoor Store

About the time sunstroke has you speaking in tongues, you're visited by the wild-eyed-but-kindly sod who desperately wants to chat because their therapist is out of town. It's also the time you start doing something interesting. You put things by the curb with a big old "FREE STUFF" sign. This is the best and most productive part of your day: giving it all away. Now you can have some real fun.

The closer to the curb your old items get, the less likely they'll be spirited back into the recesses of your garage. It also provides you with scads of instant entertainment as people screech to a halt to scoop up stuff they wouldn't have tossed a nickel at an hour earlier — the free flashlight, the lightly loved vampire costume, the popup book of toads, or that weird, potentially useful metallic shiny thing sitting there all by its lonesome.

So why not embrace the curbside concept from the get-go? Avoid the light-fingered folks, the price-complainers, and the early-birders. What you enjoy is conversation and people reusing stuff you want gone. So why not just give it away? Isn't your time what is really valuable?

On a very regular basis, I put a heaping bunch of things at the edge of my driveway and everything gets snapped up in no time. People have even taken the "FREE STUFF" sign, which I can only hope they used to carry the free stuff away on and aren't just too cheap to scrawl their own.

I am known around my neighbourhood as the guy with all the neat, weird stuff. Only at my place can phrases like "I put out the swordfish" pass without further explanation. Porch rocker moms send their little daughters along to suss out the spoils. The girls sheepishly approach, give a tentative glance, then sport a thumbs-up. They'll be back … with bags. Women always have bags. Boys like to circle, pinwheeling on their bicycles like seagulls or scraping by on skateboards, swooping in to snap up the Autobot, the articulated snake, the mangled hockey gear, or the well-seasoned baseball glove. I hear their voices echo, "Cool."

I have a regular customer, an old Chinese gentleman who is tottering into antiquity. He sports a medical mask, against the poor air, no doubt, and he materializes out of an empty street as if by Mandarin magic and fills his cloth bags. And then there's the papery, Portuguese gent whose entire English vocabulary consists of "Books fer da keeds." My friend Steve the fireman appears and clabbers together Christmas, birthday, and every-occasion presents for his two cheeky kids. As a result, I am on call for anything "Dr. Who-ish" or "Hello Kitty-ish."

Once I put out a mannequin (he looked very Parisian) who had been slumming in my garage. A lovely senior lady client of mine, who lived alone in the country, had at one point propped him up by her bay window, with his devil-may-care smile, pencil-thin moustache, and jaunty red cardigan, in the hopes that would-be burglars would be terrified by his mitten hands. But recently, she had moved to a condo in downtown Toronto and had reluctantly agreed to declutter the poor fellow. He resided in my garage until I could find him a good home. I dubbed him Snodgrass, after a dummy in an old Harry Belafonte science fiction movie I had loved as a kid. When I got him home, the poor guy fell from my back trunk like a newly whacked Soprano soldier-of-the-week. A woman walking her dog behind me was treated to the image of me punching him back in, cursing, "Get back in the bag!!" I do have fun.

I finally plunked Snodgrass down under the tree near the curb with an empty bottle of Pinot and a "FREE STUFF" sign on his boneless, splayed-out legs. I was lucky enough to be looking out the window the moment a guy passing by in a recycling truck snapped him up and, hauling him under one arm like a long-lost pal, sailed down the street, laughing hysterically. No doubt, Snodgrass was soon to become the truck's mascot, or perhaps the man's shotgun seat partner for the high-occupancy vehicle lane on the highway. I felt that this was, of course, my reason for hanging on to Snodgrass so long: to make that guy's day. I don't know why I get so tickled about stuff like that, but I do.

While working with one fellow in a downtown apartment one day, I told him we could do the Outdoor Store for him, even though he lived right off the sidewalk, with no place to leave things other than his doorstep. He was skeptical. He had a small apartment-sized washing machine, a portable TV, and heaps of stuff he meant to try and sell, but he hadn't gotten there yet and it was all blocking his hallway. I dusted it all off and put it out with a "FREE STUFF" sign. Fifteen minutes later, we went out to check, and even the sign was gone. He was astonished. I wasn't.

Any homeowner can adopt the same method of diminishing the pile of stuff that's barking their shins. Put it out. It'll be used, or fixed and used. Who cares if someone is going to resell it? You're helping your fellow man or woman as you achieve Zen. Just do it.

Think of the Outdoor Store as a friendly offering to the universe, a gentle green nod to us all. Nothing screams bargain like FREE. The rest, I drive to charities or call in my legion of ladies who have a spiderweb of charity avenues open to them: new immigrants in need, students setting up apartments, single moms, and so on.

Three statuesque and fabulously clever ladies (two of them sisters) are regular visitors to my curb, and they once dubbed my spot "The Great Outdoor Store." (Big thanks to J.J. & J.J. & K.M.) I shortened it to the Outdoor Store.

They know they can always snatch up a find: toys, books, tools, snappy clothes, doggie paraphernalia, cottage cups, garden faeries, garden supplies, things they can turn into garden supplies, old china tea cups in which to plant things, bicycles, boots, home décor, cleaning supplies, dishes. You name it, and it has appeared at the end of my driveway at one time or another. You can even Google Map Street View my address and see piles of stuff sitting there — much to my wife's annoyance. I give away a world of stuff each and every week, much of it with the tags still on.

When unclaimed items spend the night out there, I know that soon the shadows will come out to dart among the piles. By morning, there are only dents in the grass. I once caught a suit-and-tie father and his young daughter in the headlights of my car as they scrambled down the street with an old patio table I had put out. Their eyes were lit up like surprised owls. The joy of FREE.

Flash Mob Two-Step

Someday, I'd like to do one of those flash-mob things like they have on YouTube. Instead of a dance or the belting out of "Do Re Mi" in a train station, an air-horn blast would signal every neighbour on my street to strut out of their front doors with big grins and an air of purpose. Under sunshine and a blue sky, and toting boxes full of free stuff, they would wait for the horn to blast again and then would march down their driveways to the sidewalk. We'd all plunk our boxes down by the curb and wait for the horn. Another blast and we'd shift one house down, like in the game of musical chairs, and we'd dig into the neighbour's offerings; then we'd visit each house in turn, again and again. One more blast and we'd all go back home toting the new stuff, not having spent a dime. Can we all agree, once every summer, to have an Outdoor Store Street Flash Mob? We could make it a civic event.

Scrappers

Another category of stuff you can lay out for the universe to snap up is metal. And the people you want to attract are "scrappers." Every month, more or less, the city picks up big items for free to help tax payers unload any bulky belongings they are able to lug to the curb. Often, the city promotes this hurricane reality show a day or two ahead of time to entice the metal pickers, the scrappers, to roam the streets in search of free scrap metal, in jalopies kitted out with cages and trailers. They will take anything worthy of salvaging or stripping: metal, old electronics, wire. Within a remarkably short hiccup of time, even before you can retrace your steps back into the house after depositing your junk at the curb, a scruffy parade of men and women materializes to nab whatever you have left outside. It's a symbiotic way to get rid of old barbecues, swing sets, bed frames past their bounce, ski poles, cheese grinders, ancient curtain rods, lawn chairs, banged-up tool boxes, wire hangers, fridges, robots — anything metal, in fact, that has outlived its usefulness.

These people create great mangled piles of metal in the backs of their trucks, and I often wonder why their tires don't blow out sideways as they lurch away. They know a local scrap-metal yard where they turn a buck, and this is a good thing: you have someone to do your recycling and heavy lifting for you, and it is better that the wear and tear is on *their* cars and not yours. Or mine.

I love to chase after these hard-scrabble fellows and gals so I can get their cards. They've come in handy on many occasions when my clients want to thin down the garage, backyard, or wherever else metal lurks.

Spring Takeaways

The end of spring is a sad time for me, for everyone. Spring has always been about discovery, rebirth, and the chance to start anew in the warmth of summer. When it ends, I wonder what I have started, and whether or not I am on the right course. It's a hard question to pose. Are we ever truthful enough with ourselves to answer? I know I learned a heck of a lot about human nature in the spring of my career, and I wince now, like a puppy expecting a scolding, at what I still had to learn from the next season.

Spring clients taught me valuable lessons and helped me create my best techniques. I also realized it was not young families I was best at helping. There was an intangible something that I couldn't put my finger on that left me feeling empty, even though I managed wonders with some. Overall, I would come to feel the older client was the direction for me … but the why was yet to come.

The true test for me has always been summer. Summer has become my Season of the Strange. The wildest, most difficult, and most unusual clients all seem to wait until summer to bang on my proverbial door. As my business grew, summer was the testing ground for all my patience, techniques, and stamina. Let me tell you all about it, shall I?

Part Three: Summer Solstice and the Season of the Strange

In Iceland, the first day of summer comes in late April. Those of us who don't use the Old Norse calendar thankfully welcome our first summer day on June 21st. It doesn't have quite the same impact as the first day of spring. And, as June wanes, which it does so very suddenly, we lament its rapid passing. In fact, we start whining that the summer days are numbered the moment someone chirps up and says, "Hey, today's the first day of summer." As June slides out, summer slides in almost unnoticed, like a rowboat parting lake reeds.

As soon as summer is officially alight, the lazy chords of an old Donovan song begin to reverberate in my brain. Does anybody out there remember "The Season of the Witch?"

One might think this is a song featuring a wild-haired, warty-nosed woman riding a broom above an autumnal wood, silhouetted against a full harvest moon. Nope. The lyrics intone that things are strange, and I'd swear they describe the off-kilter clients I seem to get in this most heated of seasons. Summer always presents me with the toughest and most eclectic of challenges ... and the best stories. And although summer is a strange season, I love the idea that it brings me new opportunities to learn or to be exposed to previously unexplored worlds, hobbies, adventures, and people. People are like walking books to me, stories I want to read. When I see a street full of people I think, "There's a book. I wonder what page they're on or what chapter?" More than that, I love the idea that I am going to learn something. People are even more interesting in their own homes. Each client is like a new first day of school. I learn all about language and geography and life. My clients also sharpen my ability to get a huge number of things done in a short period of time. When I get into "Steve Mode," as one client called it, I have to tell my clients that while I look like a Tasmanian devil with ADHD on the outside, on the inside I am all Zen — most of the time. Ommmmmm.

A Two-Chicken Day

A client once asked me how I coped when a really tough job had put me through the wringer both physically and psychologically. What did I do at the end of the day to get my head screwed back on straight? I had to think about it. Then it occurred to me that I had developed the habit of driving to a local supermarket after a tough day and buying a barbecued chicken. Then I'd drive home and eat the whole thing, making little orgasmic moaning noises as I slump over the counter, all the while gulping away at a monstrous glass of skim milk. I'm sorry, but milk has gulpability when you're dirt tired. It's not a pretty sight, but it restores me to the perpendicular unlike anything else I've tried.

The client reflected on that quietly for a moment then asked if I had ever had a "two-chicken day." When I stopped laughing, I thought about it and realized it was a perfect way to describe the really bad ones — the Two-Chicken Days were the ones that took a chunk out of me and gave me my organizer battle scars.

That kind of day comes in fifty shades of two-chicken-ness, as you may have guessed. So, listed proudly below — complete with a Two-Chicken-Day rating system — are the top stories culled from across the Two-Chicken spectrum and from the many, many, many hundreds of homes I have landed in over the past fifteen years. They are much easier to reflect on, now, than they were at the time. Back then, they made me want to buy a lot of well-seasoned chickens.

Smile, You're on Candid Camera

Technology has offered new and exciting ways for people to keep tabs on anything in their homes. People can now remotely turn on the furnace or the alarm system, open garage doors, heat up the pizza oven, and access computers. New technology also increasingly allows homeowners a peek at their houses via tiny digital cameras that report back to their smart phone apps. I see them in the affluent McMansions I visit and the much more modest ones as well. The cameras themselves might be cleverly hidden or overtly mounted for a tempering effect. Now and then, one has the distinct feeling one is being watched and judged from a distance. The houses that make use of that type of technology make my Chicken List because of the draining effect they have on me — for a number of reasons. An organizing session, where the husband opts to watch (as well as comment on) the proceedings remotely, can be disconcerting.

One client brought me in to declutter her office space. It was also a space she shared with her husband. He was away on business, but upon learning of my impending visit, he opted, from many time zones away, to be there in spirit. The house was in Ontario, Canada, while he was in Southeast Asia, watching anxiously via Skype. It was like a webinar with a hyperactive teacher stammering out nervous commentary. I knew we were encroaching on sensitive man areas when, every now and then, we would hear a disembodied voice pipe up: "No, wait. Move the camera around. I can't see. What did you just do? Let me see," or "No, no, don't touch that. I'll deal with it … and that too. DON'T TOUCH THAT!" I felt like bringing in an exorcist. It didn't help that my client had a sense of humour and would mess with her husband by telling him we had already filled a few boxes with his stuff that we were going to sell on eBay.

I have since been in homes with cameras mounted visibly in corners, especially in kitchens, for some reason, as if the worst things always happen there. Now and then, while organizing, I swear those cameras move. Nowadays, when I know a husband is tech obsessed, I am also acutely aware that I may be on camera. It doesn't change how I work, since I've never been one to take a break from organizing a client's home to fling off my clothes and dance about with underwear on my head.

Maybe I'm just being sensitive. I know it's an increasingly odd world and folks do watch a lot of movies. It's just that trust has changed its face. In our modern world, trust is continuously verified, not given.

Two-Chicken-Day Rating: 1.25 (Because any day I feel I am being watched remotely seems endless.)

It's a Guy Thing

One day, I got a call from Alison, a friend and fellow home organizer, who had a referral for me that was a "guy thing." I braced myself. "You gotta take it, please," she said. She followed that with a nervous laugh. Alison had consulted with the potential client, a woman who desperately needed an organizer to help sort out her husband's stuff while he was out of town. Not an auspicious start.

I am always wary of "sorting out" a guy's things when he is not at home. Wives frequently ask this of me, so they can finally get some small zone of the house, long in shambles, tidied up. Though, invariably, this is what releases the Kraken and results in phone calls, at 11:55 at night, from husbands demanding to know where I put their precious staple-gun attachment or some such inane thing, just to put voice to the violation of their space. I am now supremely careful to find out, ahead of time, both who owns the problem and who owns the stuff that is the problem. To avoid those electric phone calls, I touch only what I am given permission to touch, nothing more. In this case, the husband had apparently known that something was going to be done and permission was grudgingly, sort of, kind of, given.

I'm not saying most husbands aren't perfect gentlemen. The majority are. Some even shift gears mid-visit and react positively, like the husband who didn't want me in his house and said so; however, after forty minutes of watching me transform the family's storage spaces into areas of orderly beauty, he caught me off-guard by wordlessly sliding a sandwich my way. His wife whispered, "He made it himself." Approval comes in many forms.

Many men aren't as accommodating or polite, and those are the ones who fling chickens, aspersions, and anything handy at an organizer until they go away. So, I was wary of Alison's "It's a guy thing" comment.

I made arrangements to do the session. The client turned out to be a lovely, cultured, sophisticated, and good-humoured woman whose home was a splendidly elegant one, save for the garage. This was her husband's turf and the warehouse for his hobbies. The client ushered me in to view the jumble, which, aside from the usual overstock of engine oil, scattered tools, knives, and arrows, included trophies from recent adventures in wildlife appreciation: bloodied deer feet, bird wings, and other unidentifiable remains. The killing of animals for the sheer joy of it always leaves me deeply saddened. Hacking off some part of the animal to lug back to suburban digs as a reminder of man over beast, even more so. I confess, I can't hide my aversion to this triumphant man-over-nature ritual. To me, there is no bigger self-deception than professing to enjoy nature by destroying it.

Despite that, I set to the task by giving simple definition to the working spaces and did my professional best to restore some order to the "guy thing" tangle and get things "neatified," as George Bush might have said. The client was pleased with the work and what I managed — simple order and definition of space and the sure knowledge that if they reached for a car part they would not pull back a severed thumb instead. I did, however, promise myself to never do another "guy thing" project like that again, simply because it detracts from my life and makes me so very sad to witness the undignified killing of wonderful creatures in the name of sport or honing a skill, whether it be a woodland deer or a farm-fed lion tethered to a post.

Two-Chicken-Day Rating: 1.5 (But I had no appetite for a chicken afterwards.)

I Can Hear the Chickens Calling: Bark, Bark, Bark, Bark, Bark, Bark, Meow...

Yes, I love animals. Can't you tell? And they seem to love me. I often come home sprouting more tufts of fur than an alpaca. A large proportion of the homes I organize have pets of various kinds; some have many, all running about freely — something that can prove to be a hazard for an organizer who needs to bend down, traverse stairs, open doors, reach under beds, and generally try to get things done without being jumped on, nipped, licked, leg-humped, or drooled on.

More often than not, clients don't notice their pets are underfoot or, more precisely, under my feet. Don't get me wrong. As I said, I love animals and they love me: cats, dogs, rabbits, birds, whatever beastie has full reign and run of the place is OK with me, to a point. They can be amusing, like the cat who caught his head in the strings of a plastic shopping bag (cats love getting inside bags and boxes) and ran pell-mell in every direction in an effort to escape from the suddenly inflated, crackling bag that was hot on his heels. I found him exhausted under the bed, wide-eyed and terrified. Bit of a doofus that one. Gotta love cats. Dogs, on the other hand, can fill your afternoon with the sprightly anticipation of sudden coronary arrest. Many are highly strung and ear-piercingly vocal. They explode suddenly, at the slightest movement or shadow (sometimes their own shadow), like eye-popping, epileptic warthogs released from the starting gates.

Most owners are immensely charmed and amused by their pets and love to share. Some dogs demand constant petting, hugging, and approval. Many are renowned dribblers who adore playing hide and seek with your shoes, gloves, tools, and anything else you momentarily put down. Not all are so playful. One client's dog was hugely aggressive, so it was muzzled a good deal of the time. It looked like a canine Hannibal Lecter, eyeing me with bad intent, probably imagining how well my butt would go with a nice Chianti. I learned not to turn my back on him. He ran loose at all times, making it his mission to wait until I faced the other way before generating ramming speed and plowing his wrapped snout up my derriere at twenty miles an hour. It was like having a proctology exam performed by a leather-tipped baseball bat.

One client's diminutive nightmare yapped non-stop during my four-hour visit, like a somersaulting department store toy. He never took a breath once. As the client needed the creature with her at all times, I was ready to stick a screwdriver in my head by day's end to make it all stop. I have since taken to carrying earplugs in my kit.

Studies have shown that while a cat's trilling purr has a calming effect on the human body, constant or abrupt barking can have demonstrable deleterious effects on the heart and nervous system. It's why one occasionally hears a neighbour living in close proximity to such torture shouting out windows in utter despair.

Cats are adept right-angle runners who delight in cutting criss-cross patterns full scramble across my path before plunking down right in front of me, especially on stairs, when I am carrying something awkward. Some cats are the kind you can pick up, purr to, and set safely aside, having shared a lovely little forehead to forehead bump. With others, you risk pulling back a bloodied stump. Their telltale warning *mrrrrrrrrrrrrrrr* starts way back in their throat, like a faraway ambulance, and finishes in the heartbeat just before they slice your face off.

As an aside, some clever fellow should create an alarm clock that makes that cat-being-sick-guk-guk sound. It's remarkable how the sound of a cat losing its furball lunch can hurtle you right out of bed and into the perpendicular. Still half asleep, you then scramble about to try and get to the poor beastie in time and slip the sports section underneath him before the inevitable disgorging. Usually about then, he takes his show on the road and you have to chase him about before his second round of guk-guks begin. There's always a second round. It's also about then that you notice something just squelched between your toes.

Too often, I have to be careful where I walk in a client's home as many don't get around to cleaning up the little lumps of cat stuff on their rugs or even get around to refreshing their cat's box. They apologize now and then for the smell. I thought one client had used black earth in his cat box and told him litter is much easier for a cat to dig into. He shyly admitted it wasn't black earth. It had been litter, once. He had just never cleaned the box. I can hear your throat clinching up about now. I told the guy the cat is a creature that doesn't like odiferous mess, so more than likely it had found new and more convenient places in which to make a deposit. This seemed to surprise him. I am surprised by clients who get surprised by the obvious. So, we had to play Cat Box Columbo and search out the various locations the cat had been using to do its business. We found several that were deep beneath the mounded piles of clothes, discarded computers, and the upended thises and thats in his apartment.

You are wondering now, I'm sure, at what point you do not notice your pets have been unloading in multiple locations in your home. I remember a colleague of mine (Alison, again) recalling an episode of the TV show *Hoarders* where a woman had a horrible fruit fly problem and traced it to two rotting pumpkins in her living room. "How bad is it in your house," Alison pondered, "when you don't notice you've got two rotting pumpkins in your living room?" Very bad. If you love your pets, tend to their facilities (and any errant pumpkins that are past their prime!).

Fortunately, many pets are sweethearts the whole time I am there, and I love them to pieces. I can't help hugging the creatures — the ones I consider to be trained, at least.

Two-Chicken-Day Rating: 1.0 (Since animals can both delight and torture an organizer's day, I'll be cautious and go mid-range.)

Cat on a Hot Tinnitus Roof

While we're on the subject of things to be wary of in a house, I want to tell you about some of the other hidden hazards around a typical home — the kinds of hazards only experience can clue you in about.

I have a dodgy elbow I call Manny, echoing sciatica I call the Doctor, a wobbly bursitis knee I call Jazz Man and a tender thumb that goes by the name of Jennifer. I name my injuries. Injuries are a part of life; with 20/20 hindsight, they are laughably predictable. I have time to reflect upon them as I hop around gripping a pummelled thumb and whooping, "Stupid, stupid, stupid!" Fortunately, those wee setbacks are a mere bagatelle of fun that fades like the din of a bell after a few moments of song and dance.

The universe peppers my path with these little insults, so I clue in to the potentially larger landmines that are generously strewn about people's homes. When the old war wounds bid hello to me, I nod back and remember a lesson learned; my own travelling circus of characters and aversions remind me that the average home is fraught with danger and that I should always expect the unexpected. When I drop my guard, it's usually on my foot. That's the most likely time to sustain a whack, a twist, or a whiff of something I'd rather not have whiffed. Experience is something you get only after you need it. Nothing tempers speed like caution born of experience. So, beware and remember.

Here are a few lessons culled from experience and warm regret:

- Shins turn to several tones of mauve after sudden scrapes along wider-than-expected bedframes that are cleverly draped beneath a comforter or decorous skirt. Toes also frequently splay around those unexpected centre-support bedposts, usually when you're moving fast. Wear your indoor shoes when decluttering a bedroom.

- When sweeping an arm under a bed to grab a shadowy form, you may discover it has claws and teeth and is brimming with unpleasantness. Surprise!

- One should never stretch up on tippytoes to pull books from high places on long-neglected shelves. You never forget the first time mouse poop rolls off into your gaping mouth.

- When removing screws from the underside of a dining room table ... close your mouth.

- Never offer to relocate — and transport in your car — a dead anything for a client (birds, mice, raccoons). We bury things for a reason. You'll never forget the sudden look on your wife's face, the corners of her mouth pinioning downwards, as she asks, "What's that smell?" (I once remarked to my wife that I hate the smell of rotting apples. Her quick-witted retort was "I hate the smell of rotting anything.")

- Speaking of smells ... freezers long unplugged but not emptied of turkey meat and dairy products should not be opened on an inhalation of breath, especially as you bend down to look inside. As much as I hate opening them, it's good to check to see if they are indeed empty of all contents — as the client claims — before hauling them down two flights of stairs and up onto a pickup truck: sometimes they are jam-packed with jars of rotten pickles.

- Another olfactory assault comes from all those other excellent candidates for rot, like the boxes glued by dark stains to basement floors, usually under the stairs. If you gleefully pop open mildewed flaps without a mask, a nice puff of mould is yours for the asking.

- Never move ancient daybed couches older than your client, especially the kind made of solid cast iron that switchblade out like spasmodic guillotines halfway down a staircase.

- Never move a daybed down a staircase that has paintings on either side ... framed in glass ... painted by the owner ... who is in a hurry to get past you to answer the front door so they can catch the FedEx man.

- Never attempt to untangle a long-forgotten closet full of intertwined metal hangers, alone. You may never be seen or heard from again.

- Cantilevered garage doors can be swung down by distracted clients and knock you right out. You can't hear the word "sorry" when you're unconscious.

- Garage lofts are a guy's locale of choice for storing useless wood with unyanked nails and screws that offer free belly button piercings. As well, a guy will keep a lifetime supply of old broken sheets of glass that slide freely from hidden places to take off your head if you don't duck in time. (Think *The Omen*.)

- Never move lawn darts, ladders, or garden gnomes from a loft in a garage where the client's expensive red BMW is parked. Nervous moments may ensue. (Pick any scene from the *Final Destination* movies.) Ask them, politely, to move it out.

- Never yank an innocent-looking bag from a loft while balanced on a ladder. It invariably turns out to be a solidified, gravity-sucking, unholdable, sack of cement. Every house has one as a courtesy detail.

- Never catch anything while standing on a ladder — like a bag of cement.

- Never cram anything next to an old fire extinguisher on a shelf. The resulting pyroclastic dust cloud may take quite some time to vacuum up. (And to get out of your teeth.)

- Never touch a leaky pipe if you're not prepared to mop up after.

- Speaking of pipes — crawl spaces have even lower pipes, many with butterfly screws that neatly cleave scalps. Some pesky pipes fail to budge at all upon full impact with a skull.

- Always turn off the circuit before you use pliers to unscrew and extricate the base of a broken light bulb unless you like to stutter and tap dance.

- Upon fixing a chair for a client, never demonstrate the job is done by sitting on it.

- Don't carry twirling garbage bags of broken glass any distance. Arms get tired and lower inexorably toward your shins. Remember the killer chariot spokes in *Ben-Hur*?

- Don't carry objects tucked under an armpit. They will fall out. They always do and always will, especially if breakable. Carry less. Make more trips. Full stop.

- Never move a piano with a client. Period. Never, unless you like life-long bouts of sciatica and bursitis.

All of those moments and more from my tossed salad of a life deserve, if not a name, then a nod of remembrance. Unlike the things I can't change — like the fact that dark chocolate gives me a hot ringing tinnitus — injuries are moments of incident that keep on teaching. Perhaps that's what I needed to do in the writing of this book: remember the things that gave me pause, name some, and learn. As sure as night follows day, they'll happen again and again if I'm not careful. It's something we all have in common.

Two-Chicken-Day Rating: 1.5 (Any day where I learn a hard lesson like those listed above gets a 1.5 from me. Good to know but could have done without.)

All That Jazz

My blog readers make a point of telling me they love the odd world I inhabit and want to hear more stories from my always-interesting side of the street. Every house is a learning opportunity and a way for me to help future clients. Sometimes it's the house that stands out in my mind, sometimes it's the person who lived there — his or her vibes rubbed off on every wall. On rare occasions, it's the interrelation between the space, the person, and their collections that strikes me, and I have to sit down and gaze about in silence to take it all in. That's what happened in the next house I'm going to tell you about. It was a lesson in obsession I call "All That Jazz."

One afternoon, I was contacted by a real estate lawyer I know. He is a taciturn man of a few clipped words, and he got straight to the point: his client's father had passed away and they needed to declutter and stage the family home ASAP in order to sell it fast. Once more, ASAP meant "yesterday" and not as soon as humanly possible. I believe a new acronym is needed to fill this expectation gap. Let's call it ASAHP.

He noted I had a tight window to get "all the work" done. The definition of the words "all the work" is rarely specified in a call such as that one, as if I would bolt if the client were to supply me with all of the pertinent details. Once I'm on the hook, in situ realtors usually wave a hand at "all the work" and simply say, "How long? How much?"

Real estate lawyers are very much like realtors in that they view time like an employee to cattle-prod into action, and not a pal you can rely on if you're nice to him. When the lawyer toured me through the home, it became very clear, very fast, that I didn't just have clutter to clear (and all the stuff that fell between the stuff), but overshadowing that was a vast El Dorado of a music collection to contend with — the kind of thing a rabid collector would sell his grandmother to possess. It was stunning. It included what I guessed was about 11,000 or 12,000 LPs in two separate rooms, stacked floor-to-ceiling along several walls. The vast majority of the collection was old jazz and '40s big band music, with a smattering of pop and a chuckle of country for good measure. There were albums artists had recorded before they went all mainstream — like a sultry Doris Day singing true heartbreaking tunes that were never covered again. Along with the records were thousands of CDs and thousands more cassettes, reel-to-reels, and 8-track tapes.

One room had floor-to-ceiling shelves that were filled with jazz CDs in cases, and there were zippered suitcases pregnant with copies. Apparently, the client's father had been obsessed with cataloguing every album and anthology and had lovingly noted each title with tiny, meticulous writing. There were countless rows of books and, tucked between them, many slick photos of smoky clubs filled with famous people, many with eyes softly focused from heavy doses of alcohol or drugs. Many other photos had no names recorded on them, the people they depicted lost to time and posterity, slinking into the shadows.

The largest wall was a monument of plastic sleeves and LP album edges, on shelves that were at least twenty feet long and eight feet high. Next to that was a tight little claustrophobia-inducing room, quiet as an anechoic chamber as a result of the insulation provided by records that were filed floor-to-ceiling on every wall. Selecting any one album at random guaranteed a smile — a funky illustrated cover here, a Dave Brubeck gem there, and then a mesmerizing cover portrait of John Coltrane over there. Black-and-white photos proudly displayed many artists in creative mode before their mainstream corporate labels plastered bikini-clad blond women running on a beach on their record jackets and relegated the scruffy men with trumpets to small rectangles on the back, or even hid them inside. Thankfully, iconic labels like Blue Note, Columbia, Atlantic, Decca, Prestige, Verve, and Impulse were the norm on every shelf.

Each album was a prod, reminding me of names I had forgotten about: Dinah Washington, Bea Wain, Jo Stafford, Cab Calloway, Keely Smith and Louis Prima, Chet Baker, even Spike Jones and His City Slickers. It was an exhaustion of moody subculture. I delighted in hearing so many of those oh-so-jazzy names one hears only in that musical genre — names like Art Depew, Barrett Deems,

Kenyon Hopkins, Sonny Fortune, Johnny LaBarbera, or any name that began with Toots.

The Two-Chicken test came from the double whammie about to hit me. The inheriting family members, wanting nothing to do with the collection, expected me not just to get it all out so they could list the home but also to find homes for the collection. This secondary imperative drove me deeply into a crash course in everything jazz — the finding of enthusiastic collectors, the small unexpected treasures, the sampling of jazz radio stations and feeling the vibe of DJ's and their stories of legends from the past. It was something I embraced, along with the down to earth job of decluttering the jazz man's house? Keep in mind that I also had other houses on the go and bills, bills, bills. The sheer task ahead meant I was in for a learning experience rather than an earning experience.

My time frame was the blink of an eye, as usual. No simple task. It's the kind of thing you just start. You don't overthink it. If you thought about the logistics too much, it would never happen. I just picked a spot and dug in like a pit bull in full chomp. The physical exertion mixed with the time crunch made it a nightmare of pacing. I just had at it and kept at it. I started to knee-pop walk like Popeye, lurching milk crate after milk crate filled with records up from their basement lair and putting thousands of pounds of vinyl into storage for the client. I gave away vast amounts of music and helped the client sell what we could. I charged for my time and mostly didn't charge for my time, somehow embarrassed it took me so long.

One day, I filled the driveway with knee-high piles of cassettes, 8-track tapes, and many albums of polka music and "symphonic jazz for lovers" that had wealthy dressed-for-the-Ritz socialites posed on the cover, gazing into each other's soft-focused eyes over bulbous glasses of red wine. Oh yeah, and I included hundreds of mouse-poopy records from the garage. Then I put the word out to everyone I could think of to come and get it all. Lucky passersby filled their trunks upon seeing the "FREE — HELP YOURSELF" sign. Alas, the majority of the cassettes and tapes went to the landfill. My junk guys just kept shovelling and shovelling through a snowbank of cassette tapes.

Few people race to snap up a particular technology that is either flat out-of-favour or one generation removed from the original source. Cassettes are making a resurgence of sorts in the club scene and among young guy collectors, but anyone who remembers them doesn't do so fondly. We cringe, recalling bunches of tape caught up in mechanisms. We remember having to have a BIC pen handy to rewind them manually, wrestling with the shiny, now braided, folded over, and often backward part of the tape (facing out now), so all you hear on playback is a garbled cat meow. Does that ring a bell, you folks over forty? Too many people hold on to cassettes, feeling the memory and not snapping to the fact that it is just outdated, temporary technology. Still, folks ask me to donate old cassettes, thinking someone else will absorb the same good-time vibes they experienced in a day when they felt more vibrant, free, and alive.

Clunky 8-tracks never made that grade on comebacks. I suspect cassettes, being the relics they are, will sink once more. And reel-to-reels, well, nah.

Though it took me months to get rid of it all, I did learn heaps about jazz. More importantly, I saw what an effect obsessive collecting has on a family. Worse, a collector is increasingly isolated from family as they begin to compile significant numbers with time-absorbing demands like meticulous cataloguing and searches for ever more items — time that is not spent with family. As the jazz collector's daughter noted, "We never went on a vacation unless it was to go to a convention of music collectors. It was all about the music." As a result, she hated the collection for what it stole from her and her mother and could not wait to see it dispersed after her father's passing.

Of course, an organizer can do nothing about a collection that a family has had enough of unless the collector wishes to find new ways to house it or agrees to live with less. It's simply not our battle.

Two-Chicken-Day Rating: 1.5 (I give this job a Two-Chicken-Day rating of 1.5 mostly because it was not really a single day but an overall experience I am loath to repeat.)

The Fruit Fly House

Any home I face that mixes a client's emotional trauma with an unhealthy mess is sure to be a Two-Chicken-Day formula for me. The fruit fly house embodied just such a challenge.

The dogs were already barking before I pressed the buzzer, their proximity alarms on high alert. They heaved themselves at the door, and a frenzy of claws scrabbled on the linoleum inside. The client, a woman in her forties, air blasted a staccato of curses at them, but they continued to trampoline into the air, oblivious to anything but their own froth. The outside door sucked inwards momentarily as she stepped into the winterized vestibule, with the hurly-burly menagerie at her heels. The woman, a bit glassy-eyed, stared at me dully for a moment as I held up my card and introduced myself through the screen. With a hesitant smile, she gestured me in. Within milliseconds, the dogs had nipped and generously slobbered on my hands, pant legs, and much of my nether region. I was also instantly enveloped by a dank mélange of odours similar to what one would expect from a wet moose. My guess was that the moose had also pooped himself. It was the kind of throat-gripping wonderland of smells one finds in a roadside porta-potty, where, by necessity, you take wee wasp-breaths to limit your exposure during your brief stay. I tried not to be too obvious about holding a hand over my nose and mouth as we held our consultation. I also politely refused the kind offer of a sandwich.

When a client tells me not to take off my shoes upon entering the house, it's usually an indication of some housecleaning issues, and I can't help looking down and speculating on the composition of various unidentifiable organic mounds. After the first day in this lady's house, I threw out my running shoes.

Like many in dire straits, she was selling the old family homestead and moving on, hopefully to better times. She was no hoarder, but life had been unkind and had worn her thin. She not so much walked, as drifted, in front of me, like empty clothes. As with many others I'd met doing this job, she was resigned to just getting through the day, expecting nothing from life in return, accepting the idea of letting things go, and wanting only the little bit of nice that gave her fond memories. Clearly, Domestic Archaeology could help restore some of who she had once been and might revive something for the next phase of her life.

I was being funded by the new owner, who had generously offered to pay for a professional organizer to grease the wheels of progress and transition this gentle woman out, along with a tsunami of clutter. This happens more often than one may realize, and it's usually followed by the coordination of a serious army of other specialists who are necessary for getting the job done: maid services, duct specialists, junk contractors, pest control specialists, painters, even property management people to depopulate the yard of droppings and neglected foliage full of old newspapers and plastic bags.

There was a stomp of teenagers sulking about the place and they were sneering like meerkats at the suggestion that they clean up their loose clothes, electronics, and dusty detritus. Girls have a special fondness for piles of clothes on the floor or snowbanked in closets. On numerous occasions, I have had hisses sprayed at me as if I were holding up a crucifix to vampires and not just asking politely if we can pick up all the clothes. I'm glad voodoo isn't widely practiced or I'd find my face printed up and glued to straw dolls bristling with barbecue skewers.

Boys, on the other hand, prefer everything they've ever owned tightly interwoven and evenly scattered over every sticky surface, under the bed, and popping from each drawer, shelf, and cupboard. Wandering into a teenage boy's room is like accidently stepping through the wrong door at a bad restaurant and finding yourself in the dumpster room, surrounded by odd smells and cringe-worthy, unidentifiable lumps. It gives you much the same feeling as when you wade into a public pool and hit a warm spot and wonder, just for a moment, what that's all about. Boys usually rocket from brooding silence to adenoidal high-pitched rage when you try and corner them about their tidying up. "It's not my job!" is the whine that most moms hear, more often than not, from their teenaged kids, or "Yeah, after this next level, just ten more minutes…"

Once in a great while, I am absolutely charmed to be presented with apologetic, eager teens who leap to pitch in and help their bedraggled mom, the person who is inevitably saddled with the majority of the work when it comes to getting a home ready for sale. Sorry guys, it's true. The prelude to a husband's premature departure from decluttering duty happens after they review only one or two items in the vast pile of stuff that needs to be addressed. Listen for the words "Are we done?" or "Is that it?" or "Can I go now?" He may linger a moment or two to bite his lip, tap his teeth together, and give everybody crazy eyes, but there's no doubt he will slip away to put distance between himself and further tests of his very limited patience. One husband would jut his lower teeth out, farther and farther, Wolfman style. When fully extended, like an open stapler or like the Ridley Scott alien, I knew he was done.

The husband's exit leaves the mom deflated, wishing she had a nice big custard pie to grind firmly into somebody's face. If you think this is not a true scenario, then you are not the mom.

Family dynamics are tricky things. In truth, there are numerous other issues in these situations, none of which are any of my business and all of which are out of my expertise. While I am hired to get things moving forward, I am acutely aware that, to some family members who prefer the devil they know, I represent an unwelcome change in the status quo. Teenagers are especially sensitive to unwanted changes.

At the fruit fly house, I suggested we make no attempt to extricate the possessions mingled with the garbage and organic material strewn about on the sticky floors. What was needed was a shovel and many garbage bags. I cautiously brought up the concept of coliform and *E. coli* bacteria. You don't want to get into things like rodent hantavirus or typhoid. Often, clients just accept that I am wearing a mask and latex gloves up to my elbows. I often dab vanilla on the masks to offset the odours seeping in, so that what I see around me can take on the smell of cake. It makes for an odd disconnect.

A surreal moment at this house came when I had to do battle with the fruit flies. The family had consistently forgotten to rid the kitchen of several large bags of rotting garbage. The result was a fairly well-established population of fruit flies. If you've ever unexpectedly walked into a swirling cloud of gnats hovering above a summer sidewalk, you'll know what I mean. You find you're instantly pinwheeling your arms and ducking out of the way. At one point, I held the end of the Shop-Vac hose vertically in the air and watched the little suckers disappear like dozens of tiny spaceships into a black hole. I followed this with a quick spritz of bug spray.

I remember the look of delight on one neighbour's face as he followed my maniacal progress over the ensuing days. He was an elderly Italian man who seemed to be ever-so-meticulously clipping his lawn with nail scissors. He became my cheering section. When he saw me dragging yet another bag of garbage outside, he motioned me over and expressed his approval by proffering a glass of wine — a priceless offer and much better than a chicken.

Homes like that have taught me that I have to use humour and gentle coaxing to move the whole family forward. It is especially important when you can make a connection on a very human level. The lady in the fruit fly case was so eager to start a new life that I couldn't wait to get her happily on the way to her future and me on the way to my chicken.

Two-Chicken-Day Rating: 2.0 (For the level of both physical and mental effort needed.)

Here's My Cigar — What's Your Hurry?

I don't take on clients when it becomes obvious my safety may be at risk. I am not talking about air quality or mould issues but the question of personality. One woman invited me over to take on the decluttering of her home in preparation for selling. It was an edgy divorce situation, and the air was electric with static tension. I get more and more such clients these days, and all are difficult in their own special way. Some of the divorces are amiable — relationships that just didn't work out. I feel for the children and grown-ups equally in those situations.

The woman at this particular house was intelligent, and I could see in her eyes that she was hoping for help. Her husband was not on board and was clearly going to be the biggest thorn in her side. Delay tactics and outright nastiness were clearly the order of the day. As the woman and I spoke, her soon-to-be-ex puffed away on a glistening cigar nub and trailed after us in a dark huff, disparaging every thought and suggestion on how to present the home better to make it appeal to as many potential buyers as possible. The basement, for example, had had a bad flood some three or four years earlier and had been left practically untouched in the hopes that the problem would go away. It hadn't. The situation was so desperate that chunks of drywall were falling from the ceiling above the stairs and tangled piles of rigid clothes and twisted furniture crowded the floor. Just standing in the basement and breathing felt dangerous. The main floor was no better. It was soot covered and littered with grimy tools, papers, and bags of bottles and recycling. Several windows and much of the furniture were a pale ochre colour and sticky with nicotine. At that point, I politely noted that the couple should refrain from smoking in the house because they would be alienating the greater population of buyers by doing so, since few people actually still smoke. That was the gent's limit. His patience had run out. He stepped forward, took a deep draw on the nub of his cigar until it glowed red, then flicked it at me. It grazed my chest, an evanescent spritz of red fireflies drifted downwards lazily into the carpet like spent fireworks. The nub of his cigar ended up on the rug where we all watched it smolder for a few moments.

I smiled uneasily, not knowing if the guy was about to spit or take a swing at me. It's the kind of tight rictus one may affect with a plastic bag pressed down over their face. I collected my wits, thanked the lady for her time, and left. Oh yes, I was upset. Only when I was a block away did I take a deep breath and give my head a shake at what just happened.

I have become acutely adept at picking up dangerous or uneasy vibes when entering a home. I have cancelled sessions for an assistant and myself on a few occasions because of gut feelings or outright aggressive behaviour by a homeowner. When it comes to a divorce situation, until a husband and wife have come to some understanding on a visit by a home professional, be it a realtor or professional organizer, it's simply not a place for an outsider to be.

Thankfully, a disagreeable husband will, more often than not, simply display his wishes for my speedy departure by rattling change in his pocket before putting a friendly-but-firm hand on my shoulder as he frog marches me out the door. One fellow slipped a twenty dollar bill into my shirt pocket, and when he got me outside, told me in all earnestness that he permitted my visit to humour his wife and "her" realtor. His wife was dreaming of living in a nice little place farther up north. His plan was to delay any real progress until "she got over her silly dreams." Thinking about that poor woman and her thwarted, humoured dreams saddened me for the rest of the week.

When people feel threatened by an unknown situation, I have realized that they will often eschew a fight-or-flight response in favour of the more common, and more prevalent, third option: do nothing until the problem goes away. That's the one that robs life of meaning. Life is all about change and potential. One has to embrace both with equal measures of trepidation and exuberance. So now I help make the unknowns known, whenever possible.

Two-Chicken-Day Rating: 1.75 (Because life deserves better.)

Keep Your Back to the Sun, Eh?

One young woman who called was of Mohawk descent. Her voice on the phone was pleasant, articulate, and worried that I'd turn her down. She was a teacher working in a nearby community and sharing a home with her grandfather on a First Nations reserve well west of Toronto. She yearned for a way to make her second-floor rooms far more organized and appealing. She needed ideas and physical help, not just products sold to her like many had attempted before. Her sister had hired me a year earlier, and noted that she loved the human touch I brought to my work.

The surrounding countryside was a low, flat expanse of farms, small towns, and sleepy trails of dry, hip-high sawgrass that lined dusty, winding back roads. The overall soundtrack to the day's pounding heat and blinding sun was a 1,000-bug chorus of overheated cicadas shouting, "Shi-shi-shi."

At the time of my visit, there had been some very difficult and ongoing tensions between the native population and the local folk. They were at odds over land rights and intruding golf courses. There were blockades, protests, and nastiness all around.

The lady's fear was that I would not risk the ire of the locals, or even venture out of my Oakville comfort zone, to take a job on the reserve. She didn't know I have a boundless curiosity and that I love doing something different every chance I get. Plus, in those early days of my organizing business, I took every job I could. It's the road travelled often by self-employed entrepreneurs until the grand day comes when they have a reputation and are in the enviable position of turning down work. The hallmark of small-business success comes when you don't have to drive two hours to find two hours of billable work, or when you can enjoy a quiet dinner with your wife or significant other instead of working evenings, or when you actually have enough cash to pay all your bills each month. Oh, the joy of having enough! To the client's delight and surprise, I jumped at the opportunity she presented.

The drive from the manicured dome of suburban niceness to her rural reality was an uneventful one until I realized my assumed directions were completely and hilariously off the mark. When the mesmerizing mirages of water on the paved roads gave way to a ruddy, talcum powder-like dirt that drifted in slow motion into the grass behind my car, I stopped to regroup.

I prefer open windows and the wind in my face to air conditioning — always have — but I admit, warm breezes make my mind wander, and in that brief sojourn into mind think, I got hopelessly lost. Calling the client for follow-up directions wasn't a great help as there were no real detailed maps of where I was going. To get to her, I needed to know where I was, and that was sheer mystery.

I backtracked enough to find and pull into a local cafe, the kind with tin pop signs outside and a measured pace of life inside. I told the cashier, a bit too loudly, that I was a professional organizer heading into the reserve and that I was lost and late. A nearby table of burly gents eyed me levelly. One growled suspiciously, "An organizer! Whaddaya want to go in there for?" I quickly realized my mistake and added, "Oh, not a political organizer, a home organizer. I get homes organized, decluttered, and staged for … sale. A young teacher is expecting me." I trailed off with a weak smile. The tension diffused to dismissal. The waitress took pity on me, pulled me outside, and pointed down a road.

"Take that road over there," she said. "Then over a bridge, take a left, take a right, then carry on for a few miles and you're in there." The term "in there" seemed to imply some hidden unknown of which I should be wary. She might well have said, "There be tigers." If she had kindly patted me on the head for good measure, I would not have been surprised.

The second I drove off, I was lost again. But to my surprise, I found what I was looking for, though I was an hour late. I pulled up into the driveway of an old, bedraggled homestead. It was unkempt for the most part, with no front steps. I had to actually climb up to the front door. I wondered how this lady's grandfather managed it every day. It had a lovely area of wooded land crosscut by a slim, slow-flowing river. I was greeted warmly by the woman, who turned out to be astonishingly lovely, with a remarkable cinnamon complexion, long dark hair, deep, bottomless eyes and a ready smile. Her grandfather kept his distance in the lower level, as did his large and wary German shepherd dog.

Too many people forget how a simple tidy up can bring great visual relief to a room, and they lack the organizational skills to do the work, so they simply give up and do nothing. The clutter builds up until it overwhelms a space with a sameness of undefined, uninspiring mess. What was really needed to help this young woman were a couple of focal points — clean, quiet areas of Zen to which she could escape. She needed a nice storage unit for books, some décor, and maybe a place to light a candle or two. That would help define, if not a whole room, then a quadrant of one. I learned that the family had a trailer filled with furniture in the woods across the little river. An expedition was immediately arranged to recruit new additions to my client's place of Zen. Crossing the river empty-handed was easy. The trailer was dank and filled with a number of mouldering bits of mulchy drywall and boxes. But it had a really nice armoire that would be perfect for what I had in mind.

I sent my client back to do a few things while I figured out a way to get the armoire into the house. I didn't want her lifting something heavy and thought, like an idiot, that I'd be gallant, so I set about doing it alone. I grappled with the thing and wrestled it piggyback out the door and down a small trail to the river. The heat was stifling. Hiking my pant legs up and tossing my shoes and socks to the other side, I tried fording the river without a plan or a moment's thought. A mistake. Halfway across, I realized my feet weren't as tough as I thought. Twigs and small stones dug deeply into them as if I were riverdancing on barbed wire. Twice, I almost lost my balance and my grip. I must have looked like I was carrying a fridge, it was so unwieldy. Sweat rolled down my face, but with my hands occupied, I could only blow the drops out of my eyes. About that time, I started asking myself what I was doing with my life. This was suddenly a Two-Chicken Day, and I had no idea how it would end.

I didn't have too much time to reflect on it, however, as the German shepherd dog arrived on the scene. He latched onto my pants, yanked my leg into the air and began dragging me forward in great lurching tugs. I dance hopped on one foot like I was doing a new Russian ballet. A few choice words and some desperate moments later, the grandfather appeared and whistled for the "puppy" to leave me alone. I was a ragged mess — hardly the professional I wanted to appear to be.

Then I had the task of getting the unit up into the house without steps, then up the narrow stairs to the second floor, and in place. This was one of those tests of will where you find yourself in the throes of a task with no choice but to see it through, despite all odds.

But manage it I did. A few touches to the area around the new bit of nice made all the difference to my client and her space. Her genuine, bright smile of appreciation made it all worth the effort. When it was time to leave, I knew with absolute certainty I would get hopelessly lost again. I wasn't looking forward to it. I said as much, noting that the locals had told me to take this road and that road over that bridge and so on, but I had already totally forgotten the way.

The grandfather materialized beside me and, for the first time, spoke in an ancient papery whisper of a voice, saying, "When you take that road out, keep the sun at your back, eh? You'll hit the highway in no time." I tried to complicate his directions, but he repeated, "Keep the sun at your back, eh?" I thanked him. As I drove away, I started trying to remember what road went where, attempting to backtrack. I quickly got lost. Then I remembered, "Keep the sun at your back, eh?" and turned the car around to do just that. In a few minutes, the highway appeared.

I gained a new appreciation for an old way of navigation — using natural surroundings instead of man-made ones. I also learned not to set too much store by the face value of anything; more often than not, the hidden treasures in a house are the people.

Two-Chicken Day Rating: 1.5 (More of a dog day, really.)

The Two-Chicken Day Lectures

For the past several years, I've spoken to thousands of people, all keen to hear about my world and the many stories of clutter tucked away in my experiences. I am thankful for all the libraries, charity groups, churches, specialty clubs, and corporations that rounded up such enthusiastic audiences and invited me to be a keynote speaker. They include Probus (short for Professional Business and made up mostly of active retirees); the

Retired Women Teachers of Ontario; the American Women's Club; the March of Dimes Canada; public libraries in several cities, including Toronto, Mississauga, and Oakville; the McMaster University School of Nursing; various rotary clubs; the National Council of Jewish Women of Canada; retired Armed Forces members; retired RCMP members; the Young Achievers Club of Halton; Big Brothers Big Sisters of Canada; parent–child groups; the United Way; and several churches.

I have also spoken at numerous health-and-wellness conventions, a variety of home-and-garden shows, realtor team presentations and realty board trade-show events, seniors' residences, college classes (to help inspire underprivileged people and at-risk youth to get into the work force), chamber of commerce events (including a dinner for the American Ambassador to Canada), corporate and Toastmasters events, and Professional Organizers in Canada conferences and workshops. I've also been on internet webinars, such as Rick Green's *Totally ADD*, as well as a lively show in Toronto called *Liquid Lunch.* I've also done mainstream media, like CBC Radio's *Metro Morning* and *Cross Country Checkup*, and CHCH's TV program *Morning Live*. I am planning on becoming fast friends with YouTube. Loved them all and I look forward to a whole lot more.

Giving lectures is a big part of my world. It's a great way to shake up my day, reconnect with real people, and not think about myself for a couple of hours. Almost all of my engagements go well — with laughs, clapping, hugs, smiles, and photo ops all around. But every now and then, something goes south, and I have to think on my feet — if I can get away with it. Some problems are only mild hiccups, a small error in judgment, while others have firmly set into stone a cringe-inducing, bona fide, Two-Chicken Day.

Here are a few Two-Chicken-Day lectures that I will admit didn't go so tickety-boo. I gauged them from a 0.5 Chicken Day to a full blown 2.0 Chicken day on the Chicken-Richter scale.

The Charity Event Lecture

One 0.5 Chicken-Day lecture occurred when I was booked, along with my friend Dave La Thangue (fabulous entertainer — look him up), to be the energy catalyst emcees for a fundraiser event attended by celebrity Home Guru Debbie Travis. Superb woman. She kindly lent her support to help us raise badly needed funds for abused women in our region. I was also asked to help promote her new book, *Not Guilty: My Guide to Working Hard, Raising Kids and Laughing Through the Chaos*, which I'll plug here as I did such a dismal job of it that night. I did, though, use my experiences as a professional organizer to energize the crowd into loosening their pocket books for the charity, speaking when I could about the many women in difficult situations that I have come across.

We had various events planned: an auction; a fashion show of strutting, beefy firemen; and, of course, celebrity endorsements. However, we needed more – something unexpected. Somewhere along the way, we clever lads decided to shake things up a bit and parade out an eye-catching duet on stage. We figured we'd entertain them into charitable acquiescence with song. Dave suggested one of the songs be a jazzy little number called "You Can Leave Your Hat On," famously sung by Tom Jones. Now, my friend Dave is an old hand at the game of singing and impersonations. He was up for anything. I said the song sounded familiar. He said,

"Yeah, it's from *The Full Monty*." I said, "You mean where they strip? Where are you going with this Dave? And is that choice entirely appropriate for the occasion?" He outlined his plan and made it sound so fun and unexpected, I simply could not refuse. It also presented an opportunity for me to rocket out of my comfort zone — something I urge everyone to do.

We somehow inveigled our way into borrowing two full firefighter outfits from a couple of the firemen who were there for the fashion show. I was more worried about my singing voice than doffing my duds in front of a large crowd of people who were totally unaware of what was about to happen. We entered, making a big show, and losing energy by the second under the remarkably heavy outfits. We filched water from tables as we made our way to the stage for our big number. We set it up well, with the crowd mostly ignoring our banter but then quickly rubber-necking when, in full music and song, we did the deed, brazenly pulling off all our kit, save for our multicoloured boxer shorts. (Yes, I have photos to prove it.) It succeeded in loosening up the mood in the ballroom. Unfortunately, we forgot to bring ready-to-jump-into clothes or a bathrobe for after the performance, forcing us to do a bold-as-brass stiff-upper-lip comic march of shame back up to the hotel room, as if we meant it. The trip through the crowded lobby was the best, with us giving military salutes to all and sundry. No harm. No foul — or wardrobe malfunction.

Chicken-Day Lecture Rating: A mere 0.5 (For it being a tad past my comfort zone.)

The Switching Directions Lecture

A slightly awkward speaking moment occurred when I was booked to speak to what I thought was a large assemblage of women at a local community center. I had had a certain fun talk all worked out, designed to poke fun at husbands and their organizational reticence. The room turned out to be completely and utterly populated by retired male engineers. The only lady in attendance was the good lady who booked me. In a heartbeat, I dumped the planned lecture in favour of an off-the-cuff hour on engineering and the home. As serendipity would have it, I had a big bag of little pen knives with me that I thought might have been fun to hand out to the ladies. Luckily the assembled men proceeded to spend most of the lecture cutting up and poking holes in the napkins and chatting amongst themselves, saving any need for substantive plot points.

Chicken-Day Lecture Rating: A respectable 0.75

The "Where Are You?" Lecture

A more nerve-racking lecture took place on a day in which I didn't even know I was expected to speak. It was for a delightful group of retired women teachers who had gathered for their monthly luncheon. They had booked me to speak, and initially we had been flip-flopping on the month — was it May? Was it June? I thought it was June. It was May.

That day, I was deeply ensconced in decluttering and staging a McMansion in an upscale part of my hometown, getting as ruffled as one can get with heaps to do and not enough time to do it. The norm, basically. About halfway through my day, I got a call from a dignified woman, the president of a ladies' association, who calmly said, "There are seventy-five ladies in their best finery here waiting for you to speak. Where are you?" They were assembled in a large ballroom at a local, very exalted snack-bracket golf club. It was one of those "Oh crap!" electric moments. I got her to hold the fort and promised I'd be there within twenty minutes. I never, ever, like to let ladies down. I dropped everything, dashed to my car, rushed the few miles to my house, jumped into less rumpled attire, de-grubbed as fast as I humanly could, drove to the golf course, found a spot on a sand dune of sorts (as parking was non-existent), rushed up to the ballroom, and burst in the door just as she announced my name. Her lookout had spotted me bounding across the green. I took a deep breath while they clapped me to the lectern, then I winged my way through an hour-long speech, giving it all I had, including lots of dancing about and voices. I made a modest splash, offered my apologies, then hurtled back to the home of the client, who returned minutes later to comment on my agreeable progress. (I didn't charge him for the absent time.)

Those kinds of lectures are doable with a bit of fuss tossed in for good measure.

Chicken-Day Lecture Rating: 1.0 (But I loooove to do lectures any chance I get. Call me.)

The Baffled Audience Lecture

Then, of course, there are the odd lecture crowds who, for whatever reason, don't share your chemical makeup in any way, shape, or form, and who offer you only mute menace. I often wonder about people who are devoid of humour. When they get together en masse, it's a wonder to behold, especially if you are in the spotlight and each word makes you feel as if you're wearing a potted plant on your head. You'd think I was detailing how to lance a boil and not how to declutter your life. Every informative anecdote was rewarded with tight, disapproving mouths, and silence. Arms began to cross across chests, watches were checked, and seats were vacated in search of food, coffee, and bathrooms. I actually wondered if I had accidently begun to speak another language, one that was totally unintelligible to the fifty or so attendees seated before me. An appeal for questions about the topic was met with only the hum of the rotating ceiling fans. I had no idea how to connect with the crowd. I was bewildered. Time seemed to slip; for a moment, I wondered how long I had been standing silent, staring back at them all. Maybe they thought I was a mime or some interloper, pointing out the safety exits of the musty old building we were in. I wondered why I'd been asked to present at all. Maybe I was a cheap prelude for some other chunk of the evening of which I was unaware. I got through the first twenty-five minutes of an hour-long lecture, then reluctantly surrendered, with my apoplectic apologies. Driving home I began to laugh out loud, saying to the universe, "That was some crazy … stuff."

Chicken-Day Lecture Rating: 1.5 (For an uncomfortable, inexplicable situation.)

The Flax Lecture

There is always the one day where something simply horrible happens resulting in a not-to-be-forgotten-but-wish-I-could Two-Chicken Day. I take most things in stride, but some days you just want to forget. So, I'll tell you about this one quickly and be done with it. Just don't remind me later, OK?

It was late. I was late. I was starving, and I had a long drive ahead of me to deliver a lecture on downsizing, at a posh home in an upscale neighbourhood in Toronto. The audience members were sophisticated, well-to-do ladies who loved to get together for a good talk and exchange of ideas. On any normal day, the venue was an hour's drive away from my home base in Oakville, and I had allowed ninety minutes to get there. I had just rushed to finish another very physical day of organizing a home. I hadn't had time to eat all day and was feeling a bit woozy. Even after a tidy up, I still looked like I had just lost a pillow fight. I thought I had just enough time to wolf down a bowl of cereal before I hit the road. I rushed downstairs and filled a gigantic double-sized bowl of something my wife had squirrelled away in the cupboard. I fancied it was all healthy stuff. My wife would eat handfuls of the stuff when she was home and it looked quite good. I doused it with milk, inhaled it all, and dashed out the door to hit the road. I gave it no more thought than that it was a tasty but rougher variation of corn flakes with a bit of bran for good luck. Flax cereal, yum.

When I hit the highway, I felt like a fly trapped in amber. It was a tar pit of oozing traffic. Over the next hour I tried not to watch the clock, but at the sixty-minute mark, I had to call my hosts to say I was going to be regretfully late. I wasn't sure how late. The ladies, though patient, were already assembled and anxiously awaiting my arrival. It was around the second phone call that my stomach made an abrupt announcement. "Frabble!" it exclaimed. It then rippled like a Canada Day flag. I remember saying aloud, "What the hell was that?" Then another announcement: "Brack!" This time it was followed by an uncomfortable sensation of heat in my nether regions that told me that I urgently needed to find a restroom. But stuck on a highway in snail-paced traffic, kilometers from any exit, this was not an option. I began to stare enviously at far-away fast food signs and the creeping red glow on buildings in the early evening sunset. Just then, I remembered my wife's words: "I only eat handfuls of the stuff." I knew why, now. "Brack, frabble!!" again, followed by a string of what sounded like masonic chants: "Yadda-yadda, brack, flutter, ripple, sweeee-frap!" It reminded me of my fridge, which raps and hisses and clanks forlornly to itself, late at night.

I found my way into the city, onto the street, and finally arrived at the house, which was nestled in a tree-lined, upscale neighbourhood. When I pulled into the driveway, I could see curtains rustle and expectant faces appear at the window. My first words to the lovely hostess were not "Good evening," but "Can I use your bathroom?" She was surprised, gracious, and accommodating. I'm sure they wondered whether or not to call in an exorcist judging from the otherworldly sounds emanating from the tiny powder room. A polite rap on the door, a few minutes in, was followed by a sweet voice inquiring how long I might be. It was not the elegant entrance I had hoped to make.

I eventually exited, sheepishly, and was warmly greeted by a room full of patient, highly intelligent, and gracious ladies. The topic was downsizing, and throughout my talk, I had to raise my voice, not so much to make a point as to muffle the assembled voices scrabbling about in my midsection. I also avoided any sudden movements, fearing the onset of sound effects. It's at times like these that I can fall back on my years of being in the moment, enjoy giving a lecture, and ignore my scrabbling belly. It got me through a full hour of doing my best not to fold in half like some magician's assistant. It was all followed by a lovely tea and dessert spread, which I begged off most of in favour of a preemptive retreat to take care of pressing business.

There was no doubt that it was a full-bloom Two-Chicken Day, without the chicken. Nothing like it has ever happened since. Yay. Lesson learned.

Chicken-Day Lecture Rating: A 1.5 (From the twitch it gives me remembering it.)

Lords of the Hoards

Nothing shouts a solid Two-Chicken Day like that single word, "Hoarders." Thanks to a flood of network and internet shows, almost everyone thinks they know about hoarders. Those shows barely scratch the surface when it comes to the actual feel, the vibes, the smells, the chaos. Many people who have accumulated a lot of stuff tell me they are "a bit of a hoarder," without really understanding what a true hoarder is and does. There are things that an organizer runs into that most people don't know about, things that delineate the sharp contrast between collecting lots of stuff and a hoarding lifestyle.

I'll say from the outset that a hoarder is not my first choice of client. They are difficult in the extreme, and, to anyone other than those specially trained, they can wring you out like well-chewed gum. I tip my hat to those brave souls who take on these cases on a regular basis. It is often a thankless, frustrating, and frequently unsuccessful task. If anyone typifies an organizational hard case, it has to be hoarders.

Early on in my organizing career, it was abundantly clear that if I wanted to make an honest go of professional organizing — and keep my clients — I needed to find a way to subtly help people tormented by voluminous clutter without venturing too far into the history that got them hopelessly cluttered in the first place. Delving into the past often risks shutting down the whole process before it even gets started. It risks just stirring up a big mess for nothing. Uncovering an emotional issue too soon not only impedes immediate progress but also usually means my first visit will be my only one. At some point, though, true progress can begin to take hold when the client matches decluttering with solid self-reflection. Then, ever so slowly, each item can be assessed and allowed into a trash bag.

I was introduced to my first hoarder one hot summer. As usual, it was an exasperated realtor who had reached out to find someone who could step into the role of bad cop to grease the wheels of progress toward listing. I often have to bring realtors up to speed on what they're dealing with and let them know how unrealistic their schedule is as a result. A true hoarder is grappling with a high-focus, obsessive disorder, if not an outright illness. No amount of reason or logic will alter their filtered view of the universe, unless there is a wake-up call, either from an imminent eviction or visible family deterioration.

With a hoarder, one must offer a detailed, bulleted plan with specific goals, intentions, and expectations. A realistic timeline needs to be underlined. A hoarder will often ask to meet and do a consultation outside of the home first, not wanting an organizer to see the actual site. This often leads to a good deal of sideline chat and stories that seldom leads to specifics. It is best to meet on-site and gauge right away if the hoarder's intentions to move forward are real or if this is another attempt to buy more time from some pressing relative or landlord.

A plan also helps to mitigate the inevitable hyperdefensive reaction and the absolute resistance that will surely come. Your goals must be small, as in "Today we do half of the couch." I'm not being facetious. A hoarder must address and comment upon each and every object in their home — especially perceived trash — no matter how insignificant. Every object is a battle line drawn and an opportunity to defer a decision. Each crumpled candy wrapper and every empty plastic yogurt container or pile of paper is a "treasure" or is "perfectly good" — and a reason to excoriate you for wanting to add to it to the landfill site if you hint that they might want to part with it. One must listen to the language of a hoarder. The "perfectly good" and "that's a treasure" perceptions abound, and you will be the bad guy, and they the victim, if you but ask if they would like to part with it. To them, there will always be a perfectly good, solidly logical reason why the object in question is something they absolutely need to keep, something that will instantly acquire urgent and important usefulness.

To enter the landscape of a hoarder is like stepping into an alternate universe. Nothing moves in their controlled world — not even garbage. It's like tiptoeing through a minefield. Every stair, every closet, every cupboard, every surface, every nook and cranny and hole and rafter and shelf and drawer is packed, and rooms are mounded to the ceiling with box after box after box after box, and suffocated with thick stacks of higgledy-piggledy paper. Every conceivable kind of object, broken or rotting, is to be left undisturbed. Even the accumulated dust in the home has a purpose, designed to help identify where outsiders are sneaking in to take things the client perceives are being stolen from them. The variety of things kept defies the imagination. One client kept every emptied bag of dog food he ever bought, having neatly smoothed out hundreds of them and stashed them away in a now reeking closet, along with a prodigious used pizza box collection he claimed would be perfect if someday he ever considered selling his record collection on eBay. I asked him if he would ever consider selling his collection. The answer was "No, never." Newspapers are a common "keeper" because of all the articles a hoarder means to read "someday." Removing the papers would result in lost knowledge. So, they are kept. Forget available technology or local libraries that house information. Logic doesn't enter into it. It is a personal, physical interaction at play, an incomplete action whose future is unwritten. Paper hoarders often have columns of newspapers that strain the floorboards, rising four or five feet into the air. Readers imagine I am kidding once more. Don't. I am not. Every footstep results in a slide. Often, there is a prescribed path one is asked to walk. One client took the opportunity to fill a vacationing neighbour's yard with every old bicycle, barbecue, and piece of metal he could find, along with a twenty-foot trailer crammed to the doors with stuff from another house he had once owned. I have had clients who have retreated from their homes entirely because of crowded, unusable utilities and a lack of livable floor space. They live off-site wherever they can to accommodate their obsession.

    To remove anything elicits the same frantic rebuttal: "I'll take care of that." Next item. "I'll take care of that." Next item. "I'll take care of that." Next item. Soon you become the foe as the client's agitation mounts visibly, followed by comments, like "Why are you doing this?" or

"Why can't I just keep my things?" or "I can't go any further. I need to go outside for a smoke." or "how dare you add to the landfill. That pop bottle is a perfect container. I'm keeping it." A realtor may believe such a home can be cleared up within a few days or weeks with smart, professional decluttering, but the reality is that "never" is closer to the mark.

One client filled her pockets like a marsupial with each item I questioned, guarding them with fierce determination, even smiling triumphantly at her success at thwarting my efforts to help her, even though she had called me in begging for my help. When a spouse is present, they are often deflated by each denial of progress, a progress they crave to see happen and hope an organizer will bring about.

Another client, who had initially called me in and worried I would turn her down, later tore into me for more than twenty minutes after I mistakenly tossed away a tiny piece of tissue paper without asking. She smoothed it out, and clutching it like a precious jewel, cried that it was perfectly good.

After that, she locked her front door and stood guard on the balcony, barring my re-entry and making it clear that the session was over. With grim satisfaction and an unsettling grin, she said, "You are fired!" One can only stand and absorb the red hot anger, knowing it is coming from a sadly disoriented place.

As a rule, I refuse to take any donations or garbage away from a hoarder's home. I learned early on that, by evening, the emails would begin, usually written without punctuation and in only uppercase letters, like one long visual shout. They would include a detailed list of each object that had to be returned, along with a list of items that had not been taken but which the client imagined had been.

If anything had been donated, the hoarder now required all items to be returned, and wanted a list detailing the people to whom the items had been donated, along with their addresses and phone numbers. Also, if the items in question were not returned immediately, action would be taken. It all shakes my day, as an organizer who just wants to be an ally.

I try not to put hoarding clients on the spot when asking them to decide on objects. Many TV shows will deliberately choose an organizer with an aggressively opposite personality who aggravates the hoarder to maximize drama. They will often ask the wrong questions, like "Why do you need this?" or "Why don't you throw this out?" It's an approach that guarantees resistance. It's a pressure from the outside, like a diet not to eat cake, which guarantees failure. Eventually the answer comes back as "To hell with you. I'm eating cake!" However, now and then, the shows will wisely bring in an occupational therapist who asks a better-phrased question: "If I take this away or donate it, how would you feel?" Now the client has no outside pressure, and the introspection starts because they have to admit that the anger is coming from within. As one wise old phrase puts it, "What you think is coming at you is coming from you." It's either an ancient Sufi truism or something I heard from an old radio show. Grab your wisdom from wherever you can.

In any case, that type of approach internalizes the conversation long enough for the client to consider another way of looking at things. Really, though, it's something inside, an inner turmoil or life crisis, some long-ago abandonment issue that was the big trigger and caused the fuss. It's not for an organizer to press unless he or she is highly trained and can apply tried and true techniques. One has to dance around the things a hoarder simply cannot face, at least at first. You tenderly circle the ground ahead with your mental detector in place, and you weigh every word. You'd think they would lose track of the vast collections of detritus in their domain, but they notice when even the slightest change in the landscape occurs, and they often imagine changes that they quickly blame on anyone present — like an organizer, or imagined intruders (which is more often the case).

Trust is an especially delicate issue. I often know exactly what a hoarder is thinking when it comes time for me to leave at the end of a session. When I was done working with one young woman, whose toppling collections had taken over the family home, I assembled her and her mother in the hallway, upended my tool bag on the floor, and spread out the contents. I noted politely that I had a good idea she may have been thinking that perhaps I had slipped something of hers into the bag — something she could not ever lose, something that, once lost, would justify the cancellation of any future sessions. The young woman was amazed and a little embarrassed, as that was precisely what she had been thinking. She wondered how I knew. All I could say was "Experience." She thought about that for a moment, then pointed to my pants and asked if I would empty my pockets as well. I did. To lighten the moment, I noted I would not drop my pants as well. I often opt to get a signed contract from a realtor or real estate lawyer stating who is paying for my time and when. In my experience, hoarders are often too hard up to afford to pay for the much-needed attention of an organizer; other times they simply decide they shouldn't have to pay after all, as one gent announced after a tough session.

This is why, now, I defer hoarders to other organizers. I'll do messy. In fact, I love messy, but I do not love hoarding. Call me a chicken — a Two-Chicken, in fact. Call me selfish, but all I want is a happy life. At the end of the day, I want to go home, make dinner for my wife, and tell her I had a really good day.

Two-Chicken Day Rating: 2.0 (Always 2.0 because of the sheer frustration factor.)

Summer Takeaways

I have learned to trust my instincts and refuse jobs that I sense will leave me with bad memories, or worse, that will imperil my physical and mental well-being. Forging a positive life takes effort and often means sidestepping those who would drag you down.

I have learned to take a deep breath whenever I ring a doorbell and hear the cavalcade of yips and yaps. Make friends with every furry creature and make them fast – that includes husbands. Then, hopefully, the day will go well.

A home is filled with myriad ways to get punctured, pummelled, pinched, and zapped, so watch out.

I discovered that the most off-the-wall clients taught me to be wonderfully, spontaneously creative and to come up with the most simple and useful solutions.

I look at people as I would a book and never judge the cover — at least, not until I have read a few pages.

Lectures are also a lovely way to connect with my demographic but experience has taught me to be on high alert for the unexpected need for a chicken or two.

I never assume a hoarder will have me back after the initial visit, so I do the best I can to pass along observations and ideas to help them after I am gone. I learned to step back and allow therapists to take the lead. Nothing can replace family intervention along with qualified psychological assistance. But it has been satisfying to have therapists tell me that they learned a lot while watching me work. I can't ask for more.

Epilogue: The Cat's Breakfast

The other day, my wife was reflecting on life. It had me rethinking spring changes in all their glory, the fear-laden potentials and all that "moving forward into the unknown" stuff. She said, "Whenever we move on to the next phase in life, we always look back on the old one as if it was an innocent time. But at the time, it didn't seem that way." We don't really know we've changed phases until some defining marker makes it clear: a change in job, health, or some other life goal that defines our new beginnings. Along with new beginnings, there is always a sense of something lost. Seasons are like that for me. I look forward to one and despair the passing of the old one.

OK. Having said all that, here I am fifteen years on, feeling like the cheeky monkey who has defied the odds, having stayed alive in a very out-of-the-norm profession. I do live a very, very unconventional kind of life. I appreciate that.

And when it's spring again, summer can't be far away. A light breeze just snuck its way into my office and fluttered the loose receipts on my desk, reminding me it is tax time, and I should follow my own advice and do some serious decluttering and reorganizing.

Still, I ask, *Who am I, really?* Can I say the fork in the road is the one I chose well or, like everyone else, do I have unnamed regrets? Am I indecisive? Well yes and no. The place in life at which I have arrived is still a bit of a mystery to me. One thing is certain: I've discovered a new way of thinking that has brought me a modicum of peace I didn't expect, and I want to share that. By seeing so many variations of life in so personal a manner, I've been able to get off the interstate, so to speak, pull up at that back-road café manned by a mystic sage with a wizened wink and find, to my great surprise, that he is me, or a variation of me, from some other string dimension.

I intend to keep on sharing that for two more seasons of change: autumn and winter. We still have lots to talk about, you and I. I'm especially excited about a section devoted to explaining guys to my women clients. I think they'll find it illuminating and great fun. That part alone is worth the price of admission. Look for bits of it in my blogs and articles on my website: **www.decluttering.ca**.

More and more people are taking on the mantle of declutterer, noting that if they can't accumulate a better life they can at least whittle one down. Ladies in droves are putting on their decluttering hats, some professionally. Few realize what they're in for, or the journey they are about to take. I suspect there will always be room for another one-man, or one-woman, operation, if the person is empathetic, able to make clients laugh, and does the work, despite having a dodgy thumb named Jennifer.

After I am done with organizing, or it with me, I will keep on being me and write about other passions — something about travelling in France or Japan, or about experiences I intend to have. More than anything, I'd love to be able to offer my wife the retirement she deserves, sooner rather than later. I'm working on it. Buy my book, and the next and the next and she'll say, "Thanks ever so much. Now pass the chocolate biscuits if you please."

You've been very patient. Ta to you all. Bubbles.

Acknowledgements

How do I thank all the people who inspired me when I needed it most? I am grateful for the feedback my wife, Irene, has offered over the years and glad she stopped short of panging me across the head with a pan. Tackling a single-helm business like professional organizing is no mean feat, especially if you specialize in decluttering. Survival is a triumph. It's about surviving the demands of dealing with all that stuff, as well as the emotional vagaries of large numbers of people — bent, frazzled, and weighed down by the things they own and that own them in equal measure; it's about the body-pummelling one endures, and the revealing fact that it is not, in any way, shape, or form, easy money. I survived to tell the tale. I will also continue the journey in my next book, available soon.

I want to thank the legions of daring homeowners who offered up their living spaces for scrutiny, shared their stories, and allowed me to sharpen my talents, all at the same time.

I include a big thank you to the many real estate professionals who entrusted the care and feeding of their clients to me. Extra special thanks go to the late and always wonderful Wendy Fradette, who first took me under her wing way back when I was shiny and green.

A random ramble of other realtors who have encouraged me along the way, in no particular order, include the fabulous Anita Alexander, Lynne Blott, Dianne and Mark Boot, Suzanne Botsifaras, Sharon Burton, Mary Cardamone, Claudia Chopik, Kevin Conroy, Dan Cooper, Donna Cutler, Colleen DePodesta, Kathy Van Driel, Rick David, Case Feenstra, Nancy Festarini, Joette Fielding, Fran Garrett, Natasha Eadie, Justyna Waz, Diana Galian, Belles Jean, Catherine Johnson, Carol Jones, Amy Kalinowski, Adriana Kirkpatrick, Yvonne Little, Heather MacDonald, Angie Tsopelas McKinnon, Gary McLean, Jackie Peifer, Colleen Pickett, Rob Raham, Lisa Roach, Ron Sabourin, Tara Seeber, Hilary Shantz, Kate Vanderburgh, Jeff Monsinger, and Haidan Wang. (Forgive me for not noting everyone. You know who you are.)

Let's not forget a few very talented and kicking stagers who brought me in on more houses than I have fingers to squash: Diane Black, Gloria Cravero, Colleen O'Hara, Bonnie Dell, Allison Donnelly, and Felicia Gimza.

Big thanks to Professional Organizers in Canada — its members, founders, and board of directors — for serving this growing need in everyone's lives and for having me as a director on the National Board, so I could give back a wee bit. Thanks of course to our American counterparts in the National Association of Productivity and Organizing Professionals (NAPO). Some POC professional organizers I've had the pleasure to work with, and who stand out in my mind, are Rose Ritchie, Alison King, Judi Suraci, Wendy Hollick, and one of the very few fellow dudes in the profession — the inimitable Andrew Neary of Toronto.

Thanks again to my wife, Irene, and my family for their generous and unsolicited feedback, as well as to my best friends, John Lenehan and Lorna Puxley-Lenehan (J&L). To Rick Green for his introduction and supportive nods, without which this book would not be nearly as interesting, or so he claims. A shout out thanks to Samantha Bland and Denise Chopin Santos for beta testing my early thoughts and regaling me with wild stories of their own about the many characters who have drifted through their second hand book store over the years.

A great, galumphing dollop of thanks to Susan Crossman whose editorial acumen and cattle prod enthusiasm and appreciation of my quirks made this book so much better than I had expected it to be. She is my velvet hammer. And to Iguana Books and their many talented people for moulding my passionate efforts into focused reality. Ta to you all.

Those who know Stephen have discovered a man of multiple talents and passionate dedication. He is a writer, artist, life coach, and in-demand public speaker. An escapee from the corporate world, he created a new business at **decluttering.ca** using physicality, psychology, and large dollops of humour to help people reinvent their lives by organizing their homes. His other writing projects include articles, blogs, and scripts for film and television, including a potential drama-comedy series based loosely on his organizing world. He has been seen on morning television and heard on CBC radio. He lives with his wife in Oakville, Ontario. (Photo credit: Irene Puchalski)

www.ingramcontent.com/pod-product-compliance
Lightning Source LLC
LaVergne TN
LVHW090115080426
835507LV00040B/898